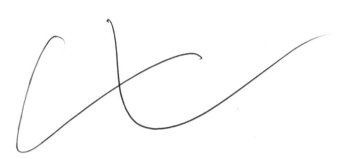

THE THIN RED LINE

THE THIN RED LINE

Uniforms of the British Army between 1751 and 1914

———◆———

D.S.V. & B.K. FOSTEN

WINDROW & GREENE

LONDON

This edition first published in Great Britain 1989
by Windrow & Greene Ltd., 5 Gerrard Street, London W1V 7LJ

Second impression 1992
Third impression 1993
Fourth and fifth impressions 1994
Sixth impression 1995
© D.S.V. & B.K. Fosten

This book is typeset in 11/14 point Bauer Bodoni
by York House Typographic Ltd., Hanwell, London
and printed by through Bookbuilders, Hong Kong

Designed by Victor Shreeve

British Library Cataloguing in Publication Data
Fosten, D.S.V. & B.K.
  The thin red line: uniforms of the British Army between 1751 & 1914.
  1. Great Britain. Army. Uniforms, history
  I. Title
  355. 1'4'0941

ISBN 1-872004-00-8

CONTENTS

INTRODUCTION

Although pioneering work has been done in recording the history of the uniforms of the British Army, there have been only a handful of attempts at producing costume plates encapsulating the dress of specific arms of service or regiments at definite periods. Other countries have been more fortunate, and enjoy a continuing wealth of such publications. Richard and Herbert Knötel, Paul Pietsch and Jürgen Olmes in Germany; Lucien Rousselot, E. Bucquoy, Eugène Leliepvre and Roger Forthoffer in France; Rudolf von Ottenfeld, Alexander Pock and Ludwig Koch in Austria; Quinto Cenni and General Gibellini in Italy — all have contributed attractive costume plates recording the history of the uniforms of their respective armies. In Britain there has been a paucity of publications of comparable quality; and it has long been our ambition to fill that gap.

The first official Officers' Dress Regulations were not published until 1822. Before that date their uniform was regulated by a series of infrequent Clothing Warrants, General Orders and Circulars; and a similar situation prevailed, for an even more protracted period, with regard to the uniform clothing of the rank and file.

We have been fortunate in having access to expert analysis of all this data; and we owe a great debt to the enormous amount of research which has been carried out in collating and analysing this primary source material by such historians as the Rev. Percy Sumner, P.W. Reynolds, C.C.P. Lawson, W.Y. Carman, Huw Strachan and others. It was they who patiently extracted information secreted in hundreds of volumes of the old War Office series of papers now stored in the Public Record Office at Kew (the WO series), together with the Warrants, General Orders and Circulars which still remain in the Library of the old War Office in Whitehall. Much of their excellent work has been published in the *Journal of the Society for Army Historical Research* and elsewhere, and we have to acknowledge their great contribution to the subject. Even so, we have found it necessary to carry out further research among the voluminous half-yearly General Officers' Inspection Reports, which generally provide unique resumés of the details of the clothing and equipment of regiments on home and foreign stations.

The staff of the National Army Museum have been very helpful in guiding further research into many rare books and items of documentation in the Museum collection; and we have also had access to secondary material from the Library, including the Regimental Histories, the Royal United Services Institute Uniform Summaries, the C.C.P. Lawson MSS notebooks, and the extensive scrapbooks.

In Britain we have a long-standing tradition that regiments each keep their own collections of papers, books, relics, historic uniforms and photographs. Although this dispersal of regimental resources can be a disadvantage in that much of the minutiae of existing uniforms, buttons, badges, crossbelt plates and the like are scattered over the whole country in many small, sometimes inaccessible museums, it has the converse advantage that such material thus comes under the direct control of knowledgeable and caring custodians who are, in the majority of cases, only too pleased to spend time in helping to solve difficult problems. Many regiments still have MSS copies of ancient Standing Orders, Regimental Dress Regulations and Orderly Room Day Books which can prove invaluable.

Assembling this information and presenting it in a condensed readable form, and the meticulous illustration of the uniforms thus revealed, has proved a delightful but demanding task. We have continually encountered pitfalls; and have had to discipline our approach to ensure not only that the details were correct, but that the illustrated figures had a 'period' appearance. Analysis of contemporary paintings and drawings underlines the fact that, to obtain a true appearance, the uniform clothing has to be shown as if cut in the authentic style of the time. It is because so much popular simulated historic clothing is not tailored correctly that it fails to convince. We have made every effort to ensure that our illustrations have a proper 'feel' for the period portrayed. In this edition the plates are arranged in chronological order; the small Arabic numerals following the Roman identifying numerals at the foot of each plate indicate, for the convenience of collectors, the original sequence of the separately published plates.

The British Army has the benefit of over 300 years of unbroken regimental tradition; and that alone is enough to make it the envy of the armies of many other nations. Most regiments have not only unique badges, but a long, evolving history of belt plates, buttons, facings, music, Colours, and a variety of ancient customs which help to bind serving soldiers into their *ésprit de corps*. The spate of amalgamations and reductions which has marked the past thirty years has done a great deal to extinguish many of these traditions; but a close examination of any modern regiment reveals a continuing affection and regard for past glories, and a genuine concern to retain as many of the ancestral ties as possible. We are proud to be able to help perpetuate interest in the historic uniforms of the Army in a way which we think it deserves.

D.S.V. & B.K. Fosten
Nyetimber, Sussex
1989

I

1751

Infantry of the Line: Grenadier Companies

In 1677, two soldiers of each company of the two then-existing regiments of Foot Guards, a total of about 34 non-commissioned officers and men, were detached, trained and exercised as grenadiers. A year later a Grenadier Company was ordered to be added to each of the infantry regiments of the Line. In June 1678 the diarist John Evelyn recorded seeing the two Foot Guards troops reviewed on Hounslow Heath, describing them as wearing 'furred caps with coped crowns'. The new headdress, which evolved into the mitre shape illustrated, was adopted due to the inconvenience of the wide-brimmed hat of the period for men required to sling their muskets on their backs and to throw hand grenades.

By 1751, Regiments of Infantry were composed of one, sometimes two battalions, each of between nine and 13 companies. The Grenadier Company was picked from the tallest and strongest men of the battalion. When drawn up for review the Grenadier Company took position on the right of the line; in action they were expected to lead assaults. On campaign Grenadier Companies were frequently detached and formed, with grenadiers of other battalions, into independent composite bodies.

Details of the distinctive cloth caps varied considerably from regiment to regiment, but they displayed certain basic characteristics. The carcass was red cloth stiffened with buckram. Its back had two vertical white pipings. The front was in the regimental facing colour, edged white and backed red. Around the base of the back of the cap was a 'turn-up' in the facing colour, with a white flaming grenade flanked by the number of the regiment and scrollwork. The front bore a Crown, worked in proper colours, over a large King's Cypher, flanked by scrollwork. The 'GR' Cypher varied in colour; the scrolls were normally white, but green, red or black when the facings were white or buff. Some white scrolls had green leaves. What were referred to in the 1751 Clothing Warrant as Royal Regiments and The Six Old Corps (1st, 2nd, 3rd, 4th, 5th, 6th, 7th, 8th, 18th, 21st, 23rd, 27th and 41st) differed in having special elaborate devices and badges on their caps. The Highland Regiment (42nd) wore black bearskin caps. At the apex of the fronts of the cloth caps were large woollen tufts, usually white or white mixed with the facing colour. At the bottom of the front was the little flap, invariably red, bearing the White Running Horse of Hanover. On the red border was the motto 'NEC ASPERA TERRENT' between white pipings. At the base of most flaps was a border of twisted stuff, predominantly green and yellow.

Officers' grenadier caps were usually made of velvet, and had more elaborate designs worked in gold and silver with coloured silks. Officers probably wore three-cornered hats on active service.

Hair was worn plaited and turned up at the back and tucked under the caps. (However, Morier

---

THE PLATE

FIGURES:

Top, left to right:
Corporal Grenadier, 6th Foot (each figure is accompanied by an enlarged detail of the regimental lace pattern). Both coat lapels are buttoned back.
Grenadier, 4th Foot; coat lapels buttoned over, except for exposed upper corners.
Grenadier Officer, 3rd Foot, carrying fusil.
Sergeant Grenadier, 4th Foot, carrying halberd.
Grenadier, 9th Foot, in full marching order, and with coat lapels fully buttoned over to the waist. Note brown field service gaiters.

Bottom, left and right:
Grenadier, 18th Foot.
Grenadier, 5th Foot.

DETAILS:

Top centre: Grenadier caps: 4th, 6th, 9th, 18th and 5th Foot, above Sergeant's sash, 4th Foot.
Centre left: Grenadiers' and Officers' sword hilt patterns, with sword knots.
Centre right: Cuff details, 18th and 5th Foot, the cuffs folded down to show different 'slash' arrangements.
Bottom centre, left to right; top to bottom:
Grenadier's pouch belt and match case, haversack and knapsack.
Grenadier's waist belt with cartridge box.
Front and rear details of Grenadier's coat, 18th Foot.
Grenadier's sword belt with hanger and bayonet.
Water flask.

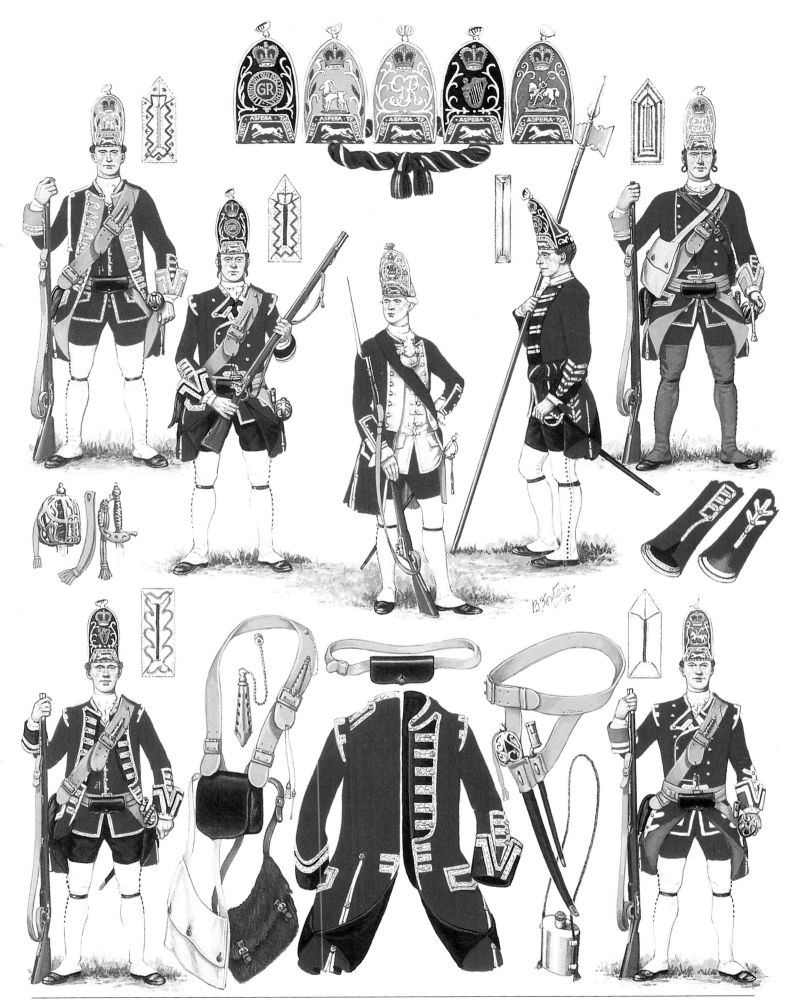

Plate I 9

also shows one grenadier with his hair worn loose and long in 17th century fashion; and another with side locks looped up in front of the ears.)

Officers' coats were scarlet with facing-colour lapels, cuffs and linings. The coats were laced or embroidered with gold and silver; and knots of similarly coloured metallic-thread cord were worn on the right shoulders. Morier shows a Sergeant of the 4th wearing a coat laced silver (as his Officers) in a style distinctly different from that worn by the grenadiers.

Grenadiers' coats were red, with full skirts hooked back. The lapels, cuffs and linings were of the facing colour; the 24th had white linings. The coat was collarless, had a red strap on the left shoulder, and in many cases red wings on both shoulders. These were ordered for all regiments except the 12th in 1752. The deep cuffs had buttoned slashes of various designs. The coat edges, lapels, cuffs, slashs, pockets, skirt vents, wings and shoulder straps were decorated with regimental lace, and the buttonholes were similarly embellished with either square-ended or pointed looping. The coat could be worn buttoned over to the waist; buttoned over but with the upper parts of the lapels folded back; or open with both lapels buttoned back.

Waistcoats were red, cut square, with two pockets, and bound with regimental lace. The buttonholes were also laced in some regiments.

Breeches were either red or blue; made with a buttoned fly, they had two inset pockets.

Officers' crimson silk net sashes were worn over the right shoulder, knotted on the left hip. Sergeants' sashes were worn round the waist, knotted on the left hip.

Gaiters were white, grey, brown or black, with about 36 bone or horn buttons. The straps were leather with brass buckles. Shoes were blackened leather of one pattern, made on a straight last rather than in right and left shapes. They laced or buckled over the insteps.

Officers were armed with a fusil, a bayonet, and a light straight sword carried on a belt worn under the coat and waistcoat. Sergeants were armed with a halberd and a hanger. Grenadiers were equipped with a broad buff leather belt worn over the left shoulder, supporting the large black pouch. The belts had brass buckles each with two pins, and brass pierced cases, by now decorative but originally, when grenades were actually carried, for the lighted 'slow matches'. (Although the grenade fell into disuse very early in the 1700s, the matchcase continued to be worn until the last quarter of the century.) Some, but not all, grenadiers are depicted with pickers and brushes for cleaning the musket lock suspended by fine chains from the loose ends of the belts. Hangers and bayonets were carried on buff leather waist belts. Hangers were of many patterns, but basket-hilted types or swords with pierced iron guards predominated. Some companies had white sword knots. Over the sword belts narrow buff leather belts were buckled to support the blackened leather cartridge pouches.

Muskets were the Long Land pattern with 3ft. 10in. barrels. Wooden ramrods were in the process of being replaced by iron. On the march cowhide knapsacks, canvas haversacks and white metal water flasks were slung over the shoulders, and the sword/bayonet belts were worn over the right shoulder.

II

c1760

15th Light Dragoons

In 1755 eleven troops of Light Dragoons were added to regiments of Dragoon Guards and Dragoons. The success of this experiment decided the formation of a regiment of Light Cavalry; and in March 1759 a Light Dragoon Regiment was added to the cavalry establishment under the command of Colonel George Eliott of the Horse Grenadier Guards. Eliott's, or the 15th Light Dragoons, was thus the first Light Cavalry Regiment of the British Army. Initially it had six Troops, each with one Captain, one Lieutenant, two Cornets, one Quartermaster, one Farrier, four Sergeants, four Corporals, 98 Privates, two Drummers, and two Trumpeter/Hornists. A year later the new regiment went to Flanders and Germany where, under the overall command of Prince Ferdinand of Brunswick, it fought brilliantly at Emsdorf and subsequent engagements.

The month following the formation of the regiment a style of clothing was approved. It comprised a somewhat shorter coat than in existing mounted regiments, with dark green facings, and white shoulder straps, lace and linings; a white waistcoat with a green collar and white cloth buttons; white linen breeches; boots with stiff cuffs and buckled-on spurs; and a red cloak with a green collar and white lining. In lieu of the ubiquitous cocked hat of the period a black-enamelled copper helmet was approved. Personal equipment was to be in tan leather.

A series of contemporary paintings confirms that, by 1760, the regiment was wearing black helmets with fluted white metal crests fronted with Medusa masks, red horsehair manes, and dark green turbans knotted at the rear, with flying tassels. The upturned fronts were embellished with Crowns over 'GR' Cyphers flanked by 'L' and 'D'. The Officers' helmets were silver-mounted and had silver tassels. Sergeants' helmets had distinctive silver or white bindings to the front parts, and large tassels. Corporals' and Privates' helmets had plain black fronts and smaller white tassels.

Officers' coats were scarlet with dark green collars, lapels and cuffs, and white linings. The skirts were not made to fold back. The buttons were silver, as was the lace, including collar loops. A surviving coat of a slightly later period offers details of the sleeve and skirt decoration. Until about 1768 Officers had silver cord aiguillettes, with silver tags, on their right shoulders, and wore the crimson silk sash over their left shoulders. Sergeants also had scarlet coats, with plain lace, and their collars, lapels and cuffs were edged with silver or white. They had silver shoulder knots; and (according to the 1751 Warrant) wore green waist sashes with stripes of the same lace as used to edge the horse furniture. Corporals and Privates had red coats with plain white lace; the Corporals had a narrow white edging to their cuffs. One painting in the collection of Her Majesty the Queen shows white loops on the collar, which may indicate some form of rank.

The equipment included a tan waist belt supporting a long tan leather cartridge box with two buttons on the flap. The belt was worn under the coat. The tan leather sword belt was worn over the right shoulder and similarly under the coat. The carbine belt, worn over the left shoulder and over the coat, was provided with a spring swivel which clipped to a ring on the 9in. long bar on the side of the carbine. This carbine was 4ft. 3in. long overall with a 36in. barrel; it had two prominent pipes for the ramrod, and a tan leather sling.

THE PLATE

FIGURES:

Left to right:

Corporal, Sergeant, Officer, Private, Trumpeter/Hornist.

DETAILS:

Top left: Officer's coat.

Top centre: Sergeants', Officers' and Privates' helmets, set over

Officers' (hilt left) and Sergeants' swords, and Officers' sash.

Top right: Sergeants' coat.

Bottom left: Privates' coat, and (below shoulder strap detail) Corporals' cuff.

Bottom centre: Privates' arms and equipment, and Sergeants' sash.

Bottom right: Trumpeter/Hornists' coat.

Plate II 29

Officers and Sergeants were armed with swords with crossbar hilts; Corporals' and Privates' swords appear to have had simpler stirrup hilts. The blades were either straight, or very slightly curved, and were about 36in. long. All ranks were also armed with pistols.

The Trumpeter/Hornists wore similar helmets to the men but with red turbans, and their dark green coats had light grey collars, cuffs and lapels. The lace was red, and the lapels bore red loops in pairs; the collars were edged with red. They also had red shoulder knots, and plain grey waistcoats. The Drummers also wore dark green coats, but faced red, with white linings. Their coats were elaborately decorated with broad white lace with a red stripe.

Captain Hinde's *Discipline of the Light Horse*, although published some years after the date covered by this plate, still provides applicable additional information.

The Light Dragoons were clothed every two years with a new coat, waistcoat and breeches; a pair of gloves was provided every year. Each Troop received a ration of four pairs of boots, complete with spurs, every year. The helmets were replaced at every second supply of clothing, i.e. every four years. New cloaks were provided when required, although it was expected that once the regiment was fully clothed only 36 new cloaks would be necessary every four years.

In 1764 His Majesty the King decided to discontinue the use of side drums in the Light Cavalry, and trumpets were introduced in their place. Each Troop then had one Trumpeter; when dismounted, these were brought together to make a Band, usually of two French horns, two clarinets, and two bassoons. When mounted they served with their Troops and used the trumpet only, although one Trumpeter had a bugle-horn of antique form which was used to sound assembly and other field calls.

The Farriers were dressed in blue, and wore black bearskin caps with horseshoe badges on the front. They had white aprons, which they rolled up on the left side, and carried axes in frogs on belts worn over the left shoulder. When the troopers were ordered to draw swords the Farriers drew their axes, placing the shaft on the right thigh, the blade towards the horse's head. They could also carry saws on the right side, supported by belts over their left shoulders; and spades, in cases on the right side of the horse, the shafts passing under their right arms.

Hinde provides a list of 'necessaries' for a Light Dragoon: A helmet, a coat, waistcoat, breeches, cloak, watering cap, four shirts, four pairs of stockings, one pair of boot stockings, black stock, one pair of leather breeches, two pairs of short gaiters, one white jacket, one stable frock, buckles for stocks and garters; and a picker, turnscrew, pick wire, pan brush, worm, oil bottle, and necessary fodder bags.

III

c1789

7th Regiment of Foot (Royal Fusiliers)

The source for this plate is a unique set of precisely draughted. highly finished contemporary watercolours in the possession of the regiment. The paintings are neither signed nor dated; but the style. and the resemblance of the details of the uniforms depicted to those of the regiment shown in the series by Edward Dayes. indicate that they were almost certainly executed in 1789 or 1790. Besides the figures shown in this plate. the set includes the Drum Major. the Fife Major. a Drummer. and an Officer. a Sergeant. a Corporal and a Fusilier of the Left Flank (or Light Infantry) Company. besides several detailed paintings of coats and various items or parts of uniforms and equipment. plus an untitled figure which is probably the Bandmaster. The figures are so carefully detailed as to be generally self-explanatory. and we need only point up several distinctive features.

Between 1789 and 1801 His Royal Highness The Prince Edward Augustus. later Duke of Kent. and destined to be the father of Queen Victoria. was Colonel of the Regiment. He took particular interest in the uniform of his regiment. and spent a great deal of money ensuring that its appointments were of the best. He produced Standing Orders which record. *inter alia*: 'All Officers are to understand that the terms ''Right and Left Flank Companies'' are fixed upon the application of what. in other regiments. are styled Grenadier and Light Infantry Companies. it being the Colonel's pleasure that. in the Royal Fusiliers. the terms ''Grenadier'' and ''Light Infantry'' should never be used . . . .'.

Black bearskin caps for Fusilier Regiments were of the same design as those worn by Grenadiers of Regiments of Foot. but were slightly smaller. The regimental badges displayed on the back parts of the caps are those specified for the 7th in the 1768 Warrant. viz. the Rose within the Garter with the Crown over it. They are embroidered in full colours for the Officer. in silver wire for the Sergeant Major. and worked in white and coloured thread for Other Ranks. The cap plates are silver plated on black backgrounds; the Officer's is of slightly different design. with bright gilded ornaments. and his cap lines are also gold. The Sergeant Major's cap has silver cords and tassels.

The Officer's coat is faced dark blue with gold lace and buttons. The Sergeant Major has a coat of similar quality with silver lace and buttons. The Sergeant has plain white. probably silk lace; and junior ranks have lace of regimental pattern. white worsted with a blue stripe interwoven. The Sergeant and junior ranks have pewter buttons. The coat collars are of unorthodox design. very carefully delineated in each of the original paintings.

The Officer has rich gold epaulettes. the Sergeant Major silver lace epaulettes; the Sergeant has similar epaulettes of white silk. and the Corporal simpler white silk epaulettes worn over the wings. The Fusilier has blue wings ornamented with oblique single bars of regimental lace. much more profuse than the six loops prescribed by the Warrant. Note that the Officer. Sergeant Major and Sergeant have regimental badges on their epaulette straps. as described above but surmounted by the grenade motif.

THE PLATE

FIGURES:

Top left: Corporal; Fusilier (rear).
Bottom left: Sergeant Major.
Centre, left to right:
Sergeant Major (rear); Officer; Pioneer (rear).
Top right: Sergeant (rear and front).
Bottom right: Pioneer.

DETAILS:

Top centre: Set over the Officers' sash. the Officers' bearskin cap (front and rear); the Officers' sword and cane; the Officers' shoulder belt plate. button, and epaulette. (Below, left

and right) Sergeant Major's and Fusiliers' shoulder belt plates.
Bottom left, top to bottom: Corporals' wing and epaulette; Sergeant Major's epaulette and sash; Sergeant Major's sword hilt and cane; Fusiliers' bearskin cap back-badge and plate.
Bottom centre: Between details of Officers' coat (left) and Fusiliers' coat, the Fusiliers' valise; Officers' glove and gorget, Sergeant Major's glove; Officers' and Sergeant Major's lace; badge worn on rear cloth patch of Officers' bearskin; Sergeants' and Fusiliers' lace.
Bottom right, top to bottom: Fusiliers' wing; Sergeants' epaulette and sash; Sergeants' sword hilt and cane; Pioneers' bearskin back-badge and plate.

Plate III 15

The white waistcoats have wooden buttons covered with white cloth. The black linen gaiters are made to fit tight to the leg and to the underside of the knee with black garters and horn buttons. They are further fixed by small buttons at the rear, attached to the knee bands of the breeches.

The Officer has a crimson silk net sash, the Sergeant Major and Sergeant crimson worsted sashes with stripes of the facing colour. The Sergeant Major's sash has distinctive and elaborate tasselled ends, which are carefully drawn in the original. All sashes are knotted on the right hip. Note that the Sergeant Major has a jewelled pin in his shirt ruffles.

The shoulder belt plates are all oval, gilded for the Officer, silver for the Sergeant Major and Sergeant, and brass for the junior ranks. The Officer's gorget is also gilded; it has a silver central ornament, and finely etched oval regimental badges in the horns. The rosettes and ribbons are blue. The sword, pouch and bayonet belts are of whitened buffalo leather, and the bayonet has a moveable frog. The black leather pouch has a plain rounded flap; lined with metal, the pouch is divided into compartments for 32 cartridges.

The Officer and Sergeant Major are armed with gilded and silvered swords respectively, both of regimental pattern. Each carries a cane, of different designs. The Sergeant is also distinguished by a sword and bayonet in a double frog, and by a cane suspended by a white strap fixed through a buttonhole on the right end of the collar.

The fiercely-whiskered Pioneer is obviously drawn from life. He is dressed according to regulation, his cap having a red-lacquered plate with white ornaments, and he is equipped with the authorised axe, saw and apron.

The Sergeant is armed with a light fusil similar to the pattern approved in 1770 for Sergeants of Grenadier Companies. The Corporal, Fusilier and Pioneer are armed with the Short Land Pattern musket.

The Officer has regimental pattern doeskin gloves with the regimental badge embroidered on the backs. The Sergeant Major has white, and the Sergeant buff leather gloves.

The artist has taken great pains to portray the powdered hair of each figure precisely, and this has been reproduced here as exactly as possible.

IV

1802

Infantry of the Line: Officers

The uniform headdress for Officers of Battalion (or Centre) Companies was the black felt hat. At this period it had reached its largest proportions and was folded flat, in the style now known as the 'bicorne'. The hat had a crimson and gold cord round the crown, which showed at the edges of the brim in rosettes or tassels. It had a pleated black silk cockade, a regimental button, and a loop in gold or silver lace according to the regiment. Officers of Battalion Companies had white cocks' feather hackles, red at the base. When attending Court, Balls or Drawing Rooms, or when their men were wearing shakos, Grenadier Officers also wore the hat, but with all-white feathers, and with a gold or silver grenade device in lieu of the button. Light Infantry Officers also wore the hat on these occasions, but with green feathers, and a bugle-horn device instead of the button.

Grenadier Officers' Dress fur caps were of black bearskin with gilt ornaments and white feathers. The caps were of similar pattern to those worn by the rank and file. Light Infantry Company Officers wore felt caps with dark green feathers and a bugle-horn badge, although contemporary drawings by Captain W. Loftie confirm that a variety of styles of headdress were worn by Officers at this period.

The scarlet coats had cross (horizontal) pocket flaps, ten buttons on each lapel, one at each end of the collar, and four on each cuff and each pocket flap. The buttons, either gilt or silver, were set on at equal distances, in pairs, or in threes, according to the regiment. The coat also had two buttons on each back skirt at waist level, and in some cases additional buttons were set in the pleats. The skirts were hooked back, and lined with white or buff kerseymere or shalloon. Skirt ornaments differed regimentally: they could be simple, or very elaborate. Lapels were buttoned over on active service, but were otherwise worn with the upper buttons unfastened, revealing triangles of the facing-colour lapels. At Court, Levees, or for Evening Dress the lapels were buttoned back. There were 'laced' and 'non-laced' regiments; the lace was either gold or silver, depending upon the regimental button metal. Few regiments had such lavishly embroidered buttonholes as those worn by the 1st Regiment of Foot, illustrated here. 'Non-laced' buttonholes were worked with coat-coloured thread twist. Light Infantry Officers wore short-skirted, double-breasted jackets, and their pockets sloped diagonally.

A gilt gorget and a crimson silk net sash were part of the Officers' uniform and were always worn on duty. Field and Grenadier Officers had two epaulettes, the latter with grenade ornaments on the straps; Battalion Company Officers wore a single epaulette on the right shoulder. Light Infantry Officers wore wings; these had laced straps, and scarlet shells edged with lace and sometimes decorated with diagonal lace bars. In the centre of the shells were raised bugle-horn badges of silver (on gold) or gold (on silver).

Adjutants and Quartermasters of Regiments of Foot wore epaulettes or wings of the same pattern as those worn by Subalterns of their units. In addition to the epaulette on the right shoulder, Adjutants

---

THE PLATE

Top centre: Officers' hat, gorget and sash, set over a shoulder belt plate of the 16th Regiment, the 1786 pattern sword, and a Light Infantry sabre. (Left) the Light Infantry cap of the 38th Regiment; (right), that of the 34th Regiment – both after Loftie. The epaulettes are those of (left) a Field Officer of the 1st Regiment, and (right) a Grenadier Officer of the 25th Regiment.

Top left: Field Officer, 1st Regiment; (below), buttonhole embroidery, turnback ornament, and gorget, 1st Regiment.

Bottom left: Light Infantry Officer, 32nd Regiment; (right) a Light Infantry Officer's wing of a silver-laced regiment, an Officer's epaulette of a gold-laced regiment, shoulder belt plate of 32nd Regiment, buttonhole pattern of 32nd Regiment.

Centre, left to right:
Grenadier Officer, 19th Regiment; Field Officer, 16th Regiment; Light Infantry Officer, 88th Regiment (India and Egypt), wearing 'round hat'.

Top right: Grenadier Officer, 25th Regiment; (below), buttonhole lace, turnback ornament, and shoulder belt plate, 25th Regiment.

Bottom right: Battalion Company Officer, 41st Regiment; (left) variations of epaulette and Light Infantry wing; shoulder belt plate and buttonhole lace pattern, 41st Regiment.

Bottom centre: Officers' coat, buttonhole pattern, and shoulder belt plate, 14th Regiment.

Plate IV 17

wore a fringeless epaulette strap on the left. Paymasters, Surgeons and Assistant Surgeons wore neither epaulettes nor wings, nor did they wear the crimson silk sash. Their swords were carried on black waist belts instead of shoulder belts.

Old-style epaulettes had embroidered straps with lace fashioned in knot-like designs. More sophisticated designs had been introduced by this date, with laced straps sometimes bearing regimental devices such as stars, and terminating above the fringe with simple or elaborate crescents. At Court or in Evening Dress, Light Infantry Officers wore the long coat rather than the jacket, with two epaulettes bearing bugle-horn badges.

The white breeches were made of fine cloth of a quality similar to the coats. They came well up over the hips and reached below the knees to the calves of the legs. Unlined, they had a small button with white tape strings at each knee, and small buttons at the rear, over the knee bands, to keep up the gaiters. Field Officers and Adjutants wore black topped boots. All other Officers were ordered to wear black cloth gaiters with small white metal buttons, but boots of non-regulation patterns were worn on occasion. On the march, or on 'out duties', dark blue pantaloons were permitted; these sometimes had black braid figuring.

The hair was queued, the ribbon beginning from near the collar and leaving half an inch of hair free at the bottom; a rosette or silk covered the tie. Flank Company Officers had their hair plaited, turned up, and fixed, with hanging ribbons.

The uniform sword was carried on a shoulder belt with a gilt or silver plate. On duty it was worn over the coat; off duty, under the coat but over the waistcoat. The straight-bladed 1786 pattern weapon had a gilded brass guard, pommel and shells, and a silver wire grip; the scabbard was of black leather with gilt mounts. Light Infantry Officers carried this sword or, more often, a sharply curved sabre with a gilt lion's-head pommel and shells and silver wire or black grip; the scabbard was black with gilt mounts. There was wide variation in details of pattern, to regimental custom or personal whim. Infantry sword knots were of crimson and gold lace.

V

1802

Infantry of the Line:
Non-Commissioned Officers and Privates

In 1800. lacquered cylindrical shakos were introduced to replace the cocked hats worn by NCOs and men. which had become unmanageably large. A modified and lighter version of this shako. made of felt and leather. appeared in February 1801: this was 9in. high. The shako was worn by NCOs and Privates of the Foot Guards and of every corps of Infantry except the Highland Regiments. Grenadiers. Drummers and Fifers were also permitted to wear the cap on occasion. The thin brass plates. 6in. by 4in.. were stamped with the Royal Cypher set in a Garter. backed by Trophies of Arms and Colours: above the Garter was the Crown. and below it the Royal Crest. It was permitted for regiments to carry their number on either side of the Crest. and those entitled to 'ancient badges' were allowed to put them in the centre of the Garter. Grenadiers had grenade motifs in addition to any badges. Tufts worn by Battalion Companies were white with a red base. by Grenadiers all white. and by Light Infantry all dark green. Regimental buttons were worn in the centre of the black cockades. excepting Grenadiers. who had small grenade badges.

The Grenadiers' 12in. tall black bearskin caps had thin brass plates stamped with the Royal Crest. the motto 'NEC ASPERA TERRENT'. the Royal Cypher. and decorative scrollwork. A white flaming grenade was worked on the lower part of the back of the cap. bearing the regimental number on the ball. The circular red cloth patch on the upper part at the back was plain except for 'Royal' Regiments. and the six senior corps. which were permitted to carry their badges worked on the patch in white. The caps had white plaited lines with tasselled ends.

The hair was worn short on top and at the sides. and dressed in an 11in. long pigtail or queue behind. Grenadiers and Light Infantry had the back hair plaited and turned up under the cap. with the ribbon ends hanging on the collar.

In October 1797 the cut of the Infantry coat was altered. Lapels were removed. and the coat became a single-breasted jacket with a single row of buttons closing the front to the waist. The buttonhole 'loops' were 4in. long at the top of the breast. reducing to 3in. at the waist. The coat was made easy-fitting and long-waisted. with short skirts cut away from the centre front in a sloping style. Sergeants' coats were scarlet. those of Corporals and Privates red. and of inferior quality. The Sergeants' lace was plain white worsted. and that of Corporals and Privates white worsted with distinguishing interwoven stripes and/or 'worms' in regimental colours. All buttons were pewter. set

---

THE PLATE

Left side. top to bottom:
Jacket. Sergeant. Battalion Company. 4th Regiment. with enlarged details of button and single width of lace.
Jacket. Sergeant Major. 24th Regiment.
Details of dressing queues. Battalion Companies (left) and Flank Companies.
Jacket. Sergeant. Battalion Company. 77th Regiment. with full marching equipment.

Centre. top to bottom:
Set over Sergeants' sash of yellow-faced regiment. 1802 shako with Battalion Company tuft: shako plate: Sergeants' sword: Grenadier and Light Infantry Company cockades and tufts: musket lock picker and brush: Light Company wing (left): Grenadier Company wing (right): Sergeant Major's epaulette. and Battalion Company Other Ranks' shoulder strap. with tuft.

Grenadier of the 19th Regiment. with full equipment.
Private. Battalion Company. 35th Regiment. in Parade Dress.

Canvas knapsack: New Land Pattern musket. with lock details.
Jacket. Sergeant. Grenadier Company. 77th Regiment. with full equipment (rear).
Grenadier cap. and back-badge.
Jacket. Private. Grenadier Company. 54th Regiment. with full equipment (rear).

Right side. top to bottom:
Jacket. Corporal. Battalion Company. 38th Regiment.
Jacket. Private. Battalion Company. 22nd Regiment (rear).
Detail. jacket skirts. Light Infantry Company.
Cuff detail.
Jacket. Private. Battalion Company. 54th Regiment. with full equipment.

Plate V 11

on at equal distances, in pairs, or in threes, according to regimental orders. Grenadiers and men of Battalion Companies had cross pocket flaps, the Light Infantry sloping pockets. Buttons on the cuffs, the pocket flaps and at the rear waist were large, on the other parts of the jacket, small; all buttons on Light Infantry jackets were small. Sergeant Majors were permitted scarlet jackets cut in double-breasted style, with gold or silver lace according to regimental orders.

In July 1802 chevron badges were introduced for Non-Commissioned Officers. For Sergeant Majors these were gold or silver, for Quartermaster Sergeants and Sergeants plain white, and for Corporals and Chosen Privates of regimentally patterned lace. The Sergeant Major and QM Sergeants had four bars, the Sergeants three, the Corporals two, and the Chosen Men (or 'Lance Corporals') one. Sergeants wore crimson worsted waist sashes with stripes of regimental facing colour, except in regiments whose facings were red or purple, where the stripe was white. Sashes were tied on the left side.

Grenadiers and Light Infantry wore red wings with six darts of lace. Grenadiers' wings were edged with a line or lace on the bottom only, those of the Light Infantry being laced on both edges. It became common for wings, and the shoulder straps of Battalion Companies, to be trimmed with drawn white wool tufting.

Breeches were white, or buff for regiments with buff facings. They reached well below the knee, and had one pocket on the right side. There was a small button with tape strings at each knee, and a button at the back above the knee band. Garters were black. Sergeants' gaiters were of black linen, those of junior ranks of black woollen stuff; they reached over the breeches to the knee and were fastened to the button at the rear, which also kept the garter in position. Buttons were pewter. White linen trousers were worn over the breeches on occasion, and for service in the tropics.

Belts were worn crosswise over the shoulders, and were pipeclayed, or ochred in the case of buff-faced regiments. Belts were 2⅛in. wide, and the plate was worn on the bayonet belt where the belts crossed on the breast. The cartridge pouch of black leather was kept in position by a narrow strap which looped around the bayonet belt behind. The cloth forage cap was rolled buckled on to the pouch. Knapsacks were of canvas, made in a folding 'envelope' style and provided with leather straps and buckles. They were painted either ochre or brown, and had the regimental number or device painted on an oval or circular patch of the facing colour on the outward face. The haversack for rations was a canvas or linen bag, usually fawn or off-white in colour, with a two-button flap, and a strap of the same material. The water canteen was of flattened keg shape, heavily made of wood with iron strapping and brackets for its leather sling, and painted blue. Haversack and canteen were slung on the right hip by Sergeants, so as not to encumber their sword hilts, and on the left hip by junior ranks.

Sergeants were armed with straight-bladed swords with brass knuckle bow guards, ball pommels and wire grips; scabbards were black with brass mounts. They were also armed with 9ft. long pikes with crossbar heads. Light Infantry Sergeants did not carry pikes; they were armed with fusils and equipped with bayonet and pouch belts. All Sergeants carried canes, and Light Infantry Sergeants carried signalling whistles on retaining chains.

The musket was the .75in. calibre New Land Pattern weapon with a 42in. barrel; but quantities of the older India Pattern musket, with a 39in. barrel, were still in use, especially by battalions with long service overseas.

VI

c1805

Royal Marines

In 1755 new Marine forces were formed on a permanent basis. At this period the uniform was red, faced white, with white linings, waistcoats and breeches, and silver Officers' lace, according to Grose's *Military Antiquities*. The Marines are also recorded as wearing caps similar to those of Fusilier Regiments, although these were probably reserved for ceremonial dress, and the day-to-day headgear was the cocked hat.

When detachments were sent on board ship it was recommended that their uniform clothing – hats, coats, white shirts, stockings and shoes – should be removed, tied into a neat bundle, tallied, and stored until required to turn them out in a well-dressed manner. Each Marine was then issued with a 'slop' jacket, a pair of stout brown gaiters, a pair of trousers, a haversack, a pair of woollen stockings, two checked shirts, and shoes, this being his sea-kit for daily use.

In 1775 it was reported in Boston that the Commanding Officer of the Marines had ordered the Officers to appear uniformly dressed when on duty with their men; and that each Officer should immediately provide himself with a jacket and a 'round hat with a silver band'. In addition, there are contemporary references to 'cropped' hats, and it seems that these were the first prototypes of the round hats which were later to be adopted as the official headdress.

In 1797 the strength of the Marines was raised to 20,000, an increase of 2,000. By 1801 it had been further increased to 24,000. Each Company comprised a Captain, two Lieutenants, eight Sergeants, eight Corporals, six Drummers, and about 120 Privates. Exceptional loyalty and service during the period of the great naval mutinies led to the Order of 8 May 1802 directing that the title of the Corps should henceforward be the Royal Marines. At about this time each of the Colonel Commandants, Lieutenant Colonels and Majors were allowed one Company with a Captain Lieutenant in lieu of one of the 1st Lieutenants. As a consequence of the change of title the facings were changed: henceforth they would be 'Royal' blue rather than 'Naval' white, and the Officers' lace was changed from silver to gold. Sergeants were to have yellow metal buttons.

Dighton, Atkinson, Carrington Bowles, etc., show Marine Officers wearing cocked hats with gold loops and tassels and white over red feathers; but there seems no reason to doubt that the distinctive round hat, which was also worn by Army Officers in many circumstances, was used by Officers of Royal Marines under some active service conditions. The hat, officially adopted for the rank and file in March 1799, was made of lacquered black felt. Until the abolition of Flank Companies in November 1804 the following distinctions applied: *Grenadiers*, brim bound black, band white, stay loops white, white worsted tuft; *Battalion Companies*, brim bound white, band white, stay loops black, white-over-red tuft; *Light Infantry*, brim bound black, band white, stay loops white, green tuft.

Field Officers had silver stars on the epaulette straps: three for Colonels, two for Lieutenant

---

THE PLATE

FIGURES:

Top left: *Officer dressed for action at sea.*
Top right: *Private in Review Order.*
Centre:
Corporal dressed for action at sea.
Field Officer in Review Order.
Private dressed for landing operation.
Bottom left: *Sergeant in Review Order.*
Bottom right: *Private in typical shipboard working dress.*

DETAILS:

Top centre: *Set over an Officer's sash, Officers' and Other Ranks' round hats, with Battalion Company distinctions;*

Officers' shoulder belt plate (top) and gorget; Officers' regulation pattern sword, and naval sabre; Officers' (left) and Other Ranks' buttons; two variations of NCOs' and Privates' shoulder belt plates.
Centre left: *Round hats, Other Ranks, Grenadier (top) and Light Infantry Companies.*
Centre right: *Cartridge pouch; Field Officers' epaulettes – Colonel, Lieutenant Colonel, Major.*
Bottom centre, left to right: *Officers' undress frock, with rear skirt details; Other Ranks' jacket, with rear skirt, lace loop, and shoulder strap details; Officers' dress coat, with rear skirt and cuff details.*

Plate VI 24

Colonels. one for Majors. Captains and Lieutenants had plain straps. Before 1804 Flank Company Officers had grenade or bugle-horn badges on the straps.

The Marines lagged behind the Army in adopting chevron badges of rank for NCOs. In an Order dated 4 September 1807. Plymouth Divisional Sergeants and Corporals were instructed to wear chevrons on their right sleeves in lieu of the shoulder knots worn hitherto.

Gorgets were gilt, of small size, with blue silk rosettes and ribbons. They bore the Royal Arms. the Anchor in a shield, and sprays of laurel. Officers' buttons were gilt. flat. with raised Anchors in sprays of laurel with 'ROYAL MARINES' above. Other Ranks' buttons had a similar design with simpler laurel sprays.

Several Officers' shoulder belt plates have been recorded. but the principal pattern is gilt. rectangular. with the Royal Crest in the centre. Almack's book illustrates two oval designs. and S. M. Milne had three oval gilt plates in his collection. All these bore anchor designs. and may have been early versions. divisional plates. or, more likely. Naval plates. NCOs and junior ranks had rectangular brass plates with the Anchor in the centre surmounted by a Crown and a scroll inscribed 'ROYAL MARINES'. with laurel sprays below. A second plate. possibly of divisional origin. is displayed in the Royal Marines Museum and was in the possession of a Marine who served at Trafalgar.

Officers' lace was gold and square-ended. and the buttons and loops were set on in pairs. Sergeants' lace was plain white worsted: Corporals' and Privates' lace was of white worsted with blue and red stripes. square-ended and set on in pairs.

Hamilton Smith shows men in white breeches and gaiters. probably laced rather than buttoned. Dighton shows white trousers for the men and blue for the Officers. Atkinson gives white trousers. white overall gaiter-trousers. and blue trousers. Grey trousers came into use later. but an Admiralty instruction of 1808 specified that all pantaloons and trousers must be blue.

Greatcoats were of the Army pattern and officially 'drab' in colour until 1813. when an Admiralty instruction specified that they must be grey.

Officers were armed with the straight-bladed Infantry style 1786 pattern sword with a gold and crimson knot. Sergeants were armed with similar swords with brass mounts. and 9ft. crossbar pikes. The rank and file were armed with the Short or New Land patterns of musket with triangular-section bayonet. The black cartridge pouches had brass eight-pointed star plates on the flaps with the motto 'PER MARE PER TERRAM' on the circlet and the Royal Cypher in the centre. During boarding and cutting-out actions there was no doubt some employment of Naval boarding pikes. cutlasses and pistols.

VII

1810-1815

79th Regiment of Foot (Cameron Highlanders)

The 79th Regiment was raised in August 1793 by Alan Cameron of Erracht under the original title of 'Cameronian Volunteers'. During the French Revolutionary and Napoleonic Wars the regiment saw active service far afield, in the Low Countries, the West Indies, Egypt, Denmark, Portugal and Spain. The 79th was in the Peninsula from 1810 to 1814, fighting at Cadiz, Busaco, Fuentes d'Oñoro, Salamanca, Burgos, in the Pyrenees, at Nivelle and the Nive. In 1815 the 79th fought at Quatre Bras and Waterloo; and it served with the Army of Occupation until 1818.

The blue knitted 'hummle' ('humble') bonnet had a diced band in white, scarlet and green, and two kinds of black ostrich feathers: 'flats', which were short, and formed an underlay, stretched over a light frame; and 'fox tails', which were longer, curled, and formed an upper layer, falling on the right side. On the left of the bonnet was a black ribbon cockade to which a Sphinx badge, inscribed with the battle honour 'EGYPT', was clipped. Distinctive feathers were fixed behind the cockade: white over red for Battalion Companies, all white for the Grenadier Company, and all green for the Light Infantry Company. A small leather peak could be tied to the bonnet on active service; and Officers had narrow leather chin straps.

Off duty and for fatigues, NCOs and men wore old bonnets devoid of feathers but with a central woollen tuft or 'tourie' on top: these were red for Battalion, white for Grenadier, and green for Light Infantry Companies. Officers would have possessed some form of bonnet, hat or cap for wear in camp, bivouac or cantonment. By the end of the Peninsular War most of the hard-to-replace ostrich feathers had disappeared from the bonnets; and they were being worn, with the peak, but with only a small company-coloured tuft or feather in front, in the fashion of the Infantry shako.

Although the 1802 Regulations are specific in stating that Officers of Highland Regiments were only to have eight buttons down the fronts of their jackets, and three on each pocket flap, the surviving jacket of Captain Thomas Bain is much more elaborate: it has twelve buttons, with gold loops, on the lapels, and additional buttons and loops on the pocket flaps.

Officers had no Undress jackets or regulation overcoats, but wore cloaks, watchcoats, riding coats, or greatcoats in grey or blue over their laced jackets when on the march or in bad weather.

All Field and Battalion Company Officers wore pairs of gold epaulettes, the former with bullions. Flank Company Officers wore gold-laced scarlet wings with silver grenade or bugle-horn badges. From February 1810 the Colonel wore on the epaulette straps a silver Crown and Star, the Lieutenant Colonel a Crown, and the Majors a Star. Company Officers had no rank badges. It is likely that the Stars were in the design of that of the Order of the Thistle.

THE PLATE

FIGURES:

Top left: *Sergeant Major; Officer, Light Company, in service dress.*
Centre: *Field Officer in service dress; Officer, Battalion Company, in dress uniform.*
Top right: *Lance Corporal, Battalion Company, in marching order; Private, Light Infantry Company, in fatigue dress.*
Bottom left: *Sergeant, Grenadier Company, in marching order.*
Bottom right: *Sergeant, Light Infantry Company.*

DETAILS:

Centre top: *Sergeants' (left) and Officers' sashes; Officers' (right) and NCOs' and Privates' shoulder belt plates; Officers' gorget; regimental cockade; turnback detail, Officers' jacket.*
Left centre: *Officers' sporran, with Field Officers' (left) and Company Officers' epaulettes; and Grenadier Officers' (left) and Light Infantry Officers' wings.*
Right centre: *NCOs' and Privates' sporran, with Sergeant Major's epaulette (left) and Battalion Company Other Ranks' shoulder strap; and Flank Company Other Ranks' wings.*
Centre bottom:
Around the Cameron sett, clockwise from top left: dressed bonnet, Grenadier; Officers' broadsword hilt; 'humble' bonnet, Battalion Companies; dressed bonnet, Officer, Battalion Companies; Sergeants' broadsword hilt; 'humble' bonnet, Grenadier Company; dressed bonnet, Other Ranks, Battalion Companies; Quartermaster Sergeants' badge; Lance Corporals' badge; Other Ranks' lace and button; Sergeants' lace and button; Officers' lace and button; Sergeants' badge; Colour Sergeants' badge.

Plate VII 5

On active service Officers wore grey trousers; some accounts give the trousers a single or double red stripe down the outward seams. Field Officers wore grey pantaloons with Hessian boots on active service, and white doeskin breeches with gold-trimmed boots for Dress.

NCOs and men wore the little kilt ('filleadh beg'); tartan cloth hose ('caddis') or tartan footless hosetops ('moggans'); short, dark grey buttoned gaiters, and laced or buckled shoes. They did not wear the purse ('sporran') on active service. The regimental tartan was a unique sett designed by Mrs. Cameron of Lochiel, mother of the first Colonel, in 1793. The Cameron sett had been considered too red to be worn harmoniously with the red coat, and the pattern finally adopted was a combination of that red Cameron with the MacDonald sett. In Review Order and for ceremonial duties, at Court, for Evening Dress and at Balls, Officers wore the kilt, purse, fly plaid, hose, dirk and buckled shoes, and Field Officers added the Highland scarf which they usually wore in place of the sash.

Officers, and Sergeants of Battalion and Grenadier Companies, were armed with brass-hilted Highland broadswords, the Officers' pattern having the Thistle engraved on the front of the guard. The swords were carried in fixed frogs on white buffalo leather shoulder belts. Field and Light Infantry Officers were armed with the sharply-curved 1803 pattern Infantry sabre, carried either on slings or in fixed frogs from the shoulder belt. Battalion and Grenadier Company Sergeants were additionally armed with the 9ft. crossbar pike, Light Infantry Sergeants with fusils and bayonets, and the latter had small cartridge pouches, with brass signal whistles chained to the bayonet belts. Corporals and Privates were armed with either the India or the Land series pattern muskets, and bayonets.

(We are much indebted to Lt. Col. A. A. Fairrie of RHQ, The Queen's Own Highlanders for his assistance in researching this plate.)

VIII

1811

Infantry of the Line:
Battle of Albuhera

This plate depicts Infantry of the Line on active service in the middle years of the Peninsular War. The examples chosen are from three historic regiments: their linear descendants, with those of seven other regiments, finally came together on 31 December 1966 to form The Queen's Regiment. All three were engaged on 16 May 1811 with Sir William Carr Beresford's Allied army at the battle of Albuhera in Spain. All three served in the 2nd Infantry Division, commanded by Major General William Stewart: the 1/3rd and 2/31st in the Division's 1st Brigade, commanded by Major General Colborne, and the 1/57th in the 2nd Brigade, commanded by Major General Hoghton. Albuhera was perhaps the bloodiest victory ever won by a British army: on 16 May 1811 Colborne's brigade suffered casualties of 58 Officers and 1,190 men, from a total strength of 80 Officers and 1,568 men; and Hoghton's, total casualties of 1,054 from 1,651 all ranks.

The 3rd Regiment of Foot, The Buffs, traced its history back to the reign of Queen Elizabeth I, when an English regiment was raised for service under the Dutch in 1572. Returning to England in 1665, it took third place in seniority in the English Line, filling the vacancy caused by the disbandment of the Lord Admiral's Maritime Regiment. The first uniform facings worn by the regiment in its new guise were described as 'flesh-coloured' or 'ash colour'. The regiment always maintained the privilege of marching through the City of London with bayonets fixed and Colours flying, which dated from its original raising from among the London Trained Bands. By the time it won glory in the Peninsula the regiment could already boast service at Blenheim, Ramillies, Malplaquet, Oudenarde and Dettingen. The 3rd (East Kent) Regiment ('The Buffs') became The Buffs (East Kent Regiment) in 1881; and a Royal Regiment in 1935.

The 31st, raised in 1702 as Villiers' Marine Regiment, subsequently served under the names of successive colonels as Luterell's, Churchill's and Gowry's (Goring's) Marine Regiment. Disbanded by 1715, it was later restored in its old seniority, but on the Irish Establishment. Returning to England after seven years, the 31st fought at Dettingen (1743) and Fontenoy (1745) during the War of the Austrian Succession. It later served in America, the West Indies, Canada, Sicily, Egypt, Malta and Italy before its arduous service in the Peninsula. The 31st (Huntingdonshire) Regiment became the 1st Battalion, The East Surrey Regiment in 1881.

The 57th, raised as the 59th in 1755, embarked for the Mediterranean as a Marine unit, it was renumbered the 57th while serving at Gibraltar in 1757, and remained on the Rock until 1763. It went to Minorca until 1767, and to America in 1775. It subsequently served at Gibraltar once more in 1804, and was shipped to the Peninsula in 1809. At Albuhera the regiment suffered some 428 casualties

---

THE PLATE

FIGURES:

Top left: *Grenadier Officer, 3rd Regiment; Grenadier Corporal, 31st Regiment.*
Centre: *Grenadier Colour Sergeant, 3rd Regiment; Sergeant Major, 57th Regiment.*
Top right: *Light Infantry Officer, 31st Regiment; Light Infantry Private, 57th Regiment.*
Bottom left: *Sergeant, Battalion Company, 57th Regiment.*
Bottom right: *Sergeant, Light Infantry Company, 57th Regiment.*

DETAILS:

Centre top: *Officers' shoulder belt plates, 57th (left) and 31st Regiments, flanking a Light Infantry Officer's sash, over which are set an Other Ranks' shako plate, 3rd Regiment; 1786 pattern Officers' sword, and Light Infantry Officers' sabre; and an Officer's gorget, the ribbons for a buff-faced regiment.*
Left centre: *Officers' epaulette, 31st Regiment, with Lieutenant Colonel's Crown; Officers' shoulder belt plate, 3rd Regiment; Other Ranks' forage cap, of a buff-faced regiment.*
Right centre: *Other Ranks' field and marching equipment.*
Centre bottom: *Field Officers' coat, 31st Regiment, with Majors' epaulette; Privates' jacket, Battalion Company, 3rd Regiment, with shoulder strap and rear skirt details; Officers' coat, Battalion Company, 3rd Regiment, with epaulette.*

Plate VIII 20

from a total strength of 647; but the survivors held their ground, and the last exhortation of their mortally wounded Lt.Col. Inglis – 'Die hard, my men, die hard!' – gave the 57th their proud nickname of 'The Diehards'. Brought up to strength, the 57th went on to fight at Vittoria, in the Pyrenees, at Nivelle and the Nive. With little respite the regiment was shipped to Canada, serving on the United States border during the War of 1812-1814. Returning to Europe after Waterloo, the 57th served in Fance during the Allied occupation. The 57th (West Middlesex) Regiment became the 1st Battalion, The Middlesex Regiment (Duke of Cambridge's Own) in 1881.

In 1811 an Infantry Battalion at full strength comprised the Headquarters Staff; eight Battalion Companies numbered from 1 to 8; and two Flank Companies, the Grenadier or Right Flank Company and the Light Infantry or Left Flank Company. Each Company was commanded by a Captain, and was composed of two Lieutenants, or one Lieutenant and one Ensign; two Sergeants, three Corporals, one Drummer, one Fifer, and between 85 and 100 Privates. In practice, however, these figures were seldom, if ever achieved: sickness, casualties, and difficulties in obtaining replacements meant that regiments were invariably under strength.

The 3rd Foot ('The Old Buffs') had buff facings, linings and belts; the Officers had silver buttons and plain, 'non-laced' buttonholes. The mens' lace was worn in square-ended loops, and had a yellow, black and red stripe. Both Officers and Other Ranks wore their buttons placed in pairs.

The 31st Foot ('The Young Buffs') also had buff facings, linings and belts, and the Officers' buttons were silver; this was also a 'non-laced' regiment. The mens' loops were square-ended, with a mid-blue and yellow 'worm' on the outside edge and a narrow red stripe. Both Officers' and mens' buttons were set on at equal distances.

The 57th Foot had bright yellow facings, and the Officers' buttons were gold; this, too, was a 'non-laced' regiment. The mens' lace loops were square-ended, and the lace had a central black stripe. Buttons were set on in pairs for all ranks.

Officers of Battalion and Grenadier Companies wore cocked hats with white-over-red and all-white feathers respectively. The Grenadiers' Dress bearskin caps had been left at the depots. Light Infantry Officers wore shakos similar to those of the Other Ranks – the lighter felt version first mentioned in the 1802 Clothing Warrant.

Field Officers wore two bullion epaulettes. Company Officers one on the right shoulder only. Only Field Officers wore badges of rank; Grenadier and Light Infantry Officers wore grenade and bugle-horn badges on their epaulettes and wings respectively. Gilt gorgets were worn by Officers on duty, but seldom in the field.

Officers and Sergeants had scarlet coats, Corporals and Privates red coats which faded to brick-colour in the sun. Officers' sashes were crimson silk net, and a special corded pattern was worn by Light Infantry officers. Sergeants' sashes were crimson worsted with a central stripe of facing colour. NCOs and men had pewter buttons. Sergeant Majors wore double-breasted coats resembling the Officers' pattern. Pioneers wore aprons, were bearded, and carried a variety of tools including felling axes. By 1811 white or grey trousers or overalls were worn by Infantry on active service, and in the Peninsula trousers were sometimes made up from local brown cloth. By 1812 grey trousers were almost universally worn, over short dark grey gaiters. Officers generally wore pantaloons with knee boots or gaiters; pantaloons were white, buff, grey, blue, or of various local homespuns.

Officers were armed with the straight-bladed 1786 pattern sword, the Light Infantry preferring the 1803 pattern sabre. Sergeants of Battalion and Grenadier Companies were armed with 9ft. crossbar pikes and swords; Light Infantry Sergeants had fusils and bayonets; and junior ranks were armed with muskets of the India or New Land patterns, and bayonets.

IX

1812-1815

Infantry of the Line: Officers

In the spring of 1812 a new pattern of shako was introduced. Officers, who had previously worn the cocked hat on service, took the new cap into use for both service and day-to-day wear. The cocked hat, in reduced form, was reserved for attendance at Court and Balls.

The shako, which became known as the 'Belgic' or subsequently the 'Waterloo' pattern, had a copper gilt plate bearing the Crown, royal Cypher, and in most cases the regimental number and any special badges, the latter in some cases being applied in silver. The cord and tassels were of mixed gold and crimson, but in green for some Light Infantry Companies. Plumes, worn fixed behind a cockade on the left side, were white over red for Battalion Companies, all white for Grenadier Companies, and green for Light Infantry Companies. In 1814 Light Infantry Companies and Regiments were ordered to wear bugle-horn badges with regimental numbers beneath, in place of shako plates. All ranks of Light Infantry Regiments, and the 28th Foot, seem to have continued to wear the 1801/1802 cylindrical felt shako (or an essentially identical improved version) as a distinction, with plume at the front, the 28th with special cut-out badges and scrolls on the front and the regimental back-badge. Fusiliers wore shakos on service: their Battalion Companies had all white plumes, the Left Flank Companies green. Grenadier and Fusilier Officers retained bearskin caps for Dress. Black oilskin shako covers were used on service and in inclement weather.

From 1811, Officers wore scarlet jackets instead of long-skirted coats, which were retained for wear only at Court and for similar occasions. Light Infantry had sloping pockets, and most other Officers horizontal pockets. Besides the facings, regimental distinctions were provided by gilded or silver buttons set on equally, in pairs, or in threes, according to regiment. Some regiments had richly laced jackets with lace buttonhole loops matching the button colour: other units had plain unlaced jackets. (In the field, Officers of some laced regiments wore plainer, unlaced jackets.)

Battalion Company Officers wore bullion epaulettes on the right shoulder only; Field Officers wore epaulettes on both shoulders. Grenadier, Fusilier and Light Infantry Officers wore laced scarlet wings. Field Officers of Light Infantry and Fusilier Regiments wore epaulettes over the wings. In most Line Regiments, the Adjutant wore a Subaltern's epaulette on the right shoulder and a fringeless epaulette strap on the left. Adjutants of Fusilier and Light Infantry Regiments wore wings. In some units Star badges of regimental design were worn on the epaulettes by some Company Officers, and in addition to rank badges by Field Officers.

Gilt gorgets with facing-colour ribbons and rosettes were worn on duty, though seldom when on active service in the field. Officers had crimson silk net sashes, knotted on the left, and Light Infantry Officers had corded sashes with tassels knotted in front. Gloves were of white leather.

THE PLATE

FIGURES:

Top left: Field Officer, 26th Regiment, Review Order.
Centre: Grenadier Officer, 28th Regiment (after portrait of Captain Cadell); Field Officer, 4th Regiment, in Dress; Field Officer, 52nd Light Infantry Regiment, Service Dress.
Top right: Grenadier Officer, 69th Regiment, Marching Order.
Bottom left: Light Infantry Officer, 33rd Regiment, Guard Order.
Bottom right: Battalion Company Officer, 32nd Regiment, Walking-Out Dress.

DETAILS:

Centre top: Set over the Light Infantry sash, the shako plate (without regimental number or device); the 1786 pattern sword, and a Light Infantry sabre; the 1812 shako dressed for (left to right) Grenadier, Battalion, and Light Infantry Companies.
Left and right centre: Shoulder belt plates and buttons of the regiments illustrated in the figures.
Centre bottom: Below a selection of shako plates with regimental numbers and devices, the jacket (left) of an Officer of the 37th Regiment, with associated epaulette, button and shoulder belt plate; and (right) that of an Officer of the 81st Regiment, with Light Infantry wing, shoulder belt plate and button.

On Field Days and Active Service, in Marching Order, and when on day-to-day duties in bivouacs and cantonments grey trousers were worn; in Review Order and on ceremonial or social occasions white pantaloons were worn with boots. In some regiments coloured pantaloons were permitted for Balls, etc. Some pantaloons were decorated with fancy silver or gold lace embellishments, and grey trousers were sometimes decorated with lace stripes on the outward seams, and leather strapping and cuffs. In 1811 the caped, double-breasted grey greatcoat was introduced.

Grenadier and Battalion Company Officers were armed with the 1786 pattern sword, silver-mounted in some regiments. Light Infantry, and some Grenadier and Fusilier Officers were armed with sabres. Field Officers and Adjutants, when mounted, were equipped with waist belts and slings. Sword knots were of gold and crimson, and scabbards of black leather with gilded or silvered mounts.

An extract from the regimental standing orders of the 29th Regiment of Foot, issued on 24 June 1812, provides additional details of representative practices. For example, on home service Field Officers and the Adjutant were ordered to appear in white web breeches, high boots and spurs. All other Officers were to parade in white pantaloons and half-boots. However, at all Reviews and special ceremonial parades they were to appear in black cloth leggins and white breeches, the former to come well up to the kneecap, with only two of the breeches buttons exposed above them. Gorgets were to be worn for all Reviews, Field Days, Marches, and public and regimental duties, and were fastened 'to the stock' with ribbons and rosettes. The top three buttons of the jacket lapels were left undone, the lapels folded back and the shirt frill worn outside. Sashes were always to be tied on the left side. The shakos (called 'caps') were to be worn perfectly straight on the head. When paying compliments the Officer was never to remove his cap, but to bring the right hand over the peak. Upon active service and on marches and fatigue duties grey pantaloon overalls were to be worn, having six buttons opening at the bottom.

X

1812-1815

Infantry of the Line: Flank Companies: Non-Commissioned Officers and Privates

From 1802 to 1812 the NCOs and Privates of the Line wore cylindrical shakos, originally of leather and subsequently of felt. These 'caps' were never comfortable; they gave indifferent protection from the weather, and were hard to keep on the head. In June 1811 they were condemned by the Board of General Officers responsible for clothing the Army; a new model was subsequently submitted, and approved. Issue began at some point after the spring of 1812. It was worn in the Waterloo campaign of 1815, and probably in America and Canada during the War of 1812-1814, but it is unlikely to have been issued in any numbers, if at all, in the Peninsula.

It was worn by all ranks of the Light Infantry and Grenadier Companies of Regiments of Infantry of the Line, the latter retaining their bearskin caps for ceremonial occasions. The felt cap was roughly cylindrical, the top being about 7in. in diameter, and the slightly in-sloped rear elevation being about 6¾in. high. The front, which was raised above the level of the top surface, was 8¾in. high, and the edge was bound with ⅜in. black ribbed braid. In some examples there was a further braid binding around the bottom edge of the cap. The flat peak was 2¼in. deep. At the rear of the cap many examples had a rectangular oilskin 'fall', a neck-flap caught up with hooks and eyes when not in use.

The garland was of white worsted cord, with tasselled ends on the right. Some Light Infantry Companies wore green garlands. The tuft was fixed on the left side, in a socket behind a black cord or leather cockade, in the centre of which was fixed a bugle-horn or flaming grenade device, according to the Company. The tufts were all white for Grenadier, all green for Light Infantry Companies. The universal plate worn on the 1812 shako measured 5½in. deep by 3¾in. wide; of brass, it bore in the centre a large Royal Cypher, and in some regiments additional distinctions in the form of regimental numbers, badges, grenades or bugle-horns. The Light Infantry Companies of some regiments wore, in place of the universal plate, a cut-out brass bugle-horn above cut-out regimental numbers. Oilcloth covers for the shako and tuft were worn in the field and in bad weather; and some regiments added straps or ribbon tapes to fasten under the chin.

For full dress, normally limited to home service and large overseas garrisons, Grenadiers wore their black bearskin caps. These had brass plates, small leather peaks, white worsted tasselled

---

THE PLATE

Left, top to bottom:
Jacket and lace detail, Sergeant, Grenadier Company, 5th Regiment.
Jacket, lace and rear skirt detail, Corporal, Grenadier Company, 12th Regiment, full marching equipment.
Jacket, lace and wing detail, Sergeant, Grenadier Company, 25th Regiment, full marching equipment.

Centre, top to bottom:
The 1812 shako with (left) Grenadier and (right) Light Infantry Company distinctions, and detail of Grenadier and alternative Light Infantry garlands and cockades; within a Sergeants' sash of a regiment with yellow facings, the universal shako plate without regimental distinctions; (left) Sergeants' shoulder belt, sword, and Light Infantry Sergeants' whistle and chain; (right) Other Ranks' bayonet belt, bayonet, picker and brush.

Sergeant, Grenadier Company, 2nd Regiment, Full Dress.
Sergeant, Light Infantry Company, 53rd Regiment, Service Dress.

Rear jacket detail, lace detail, marching equipment, Sergeant, Grenadier Company, 54th Regiment.
Between front and rear views, Grenadier cap, 8th Regiment; rear jacket detail, lace detail, and marching equipment, Private, Grenadier Company, 62nd Regiment.
Rear jacket detail, lace detail, marching equipment, Sergeant, Light Infantry Company, 58th Regiment.

Right, top to bottom:
Jacket and lace detail, Sergeant, Light Infantry Company, 35th Regiment.
Jacket, lace, and rear skirt detail, Private, Light Infantry Company, 40th Regiment. (In action the musket sling was sometimes buckled round the waist to steady the equipment belts.)
Jacket, lace and wing detail, Sergeant, Light Infantry Company, 47th Regiment.

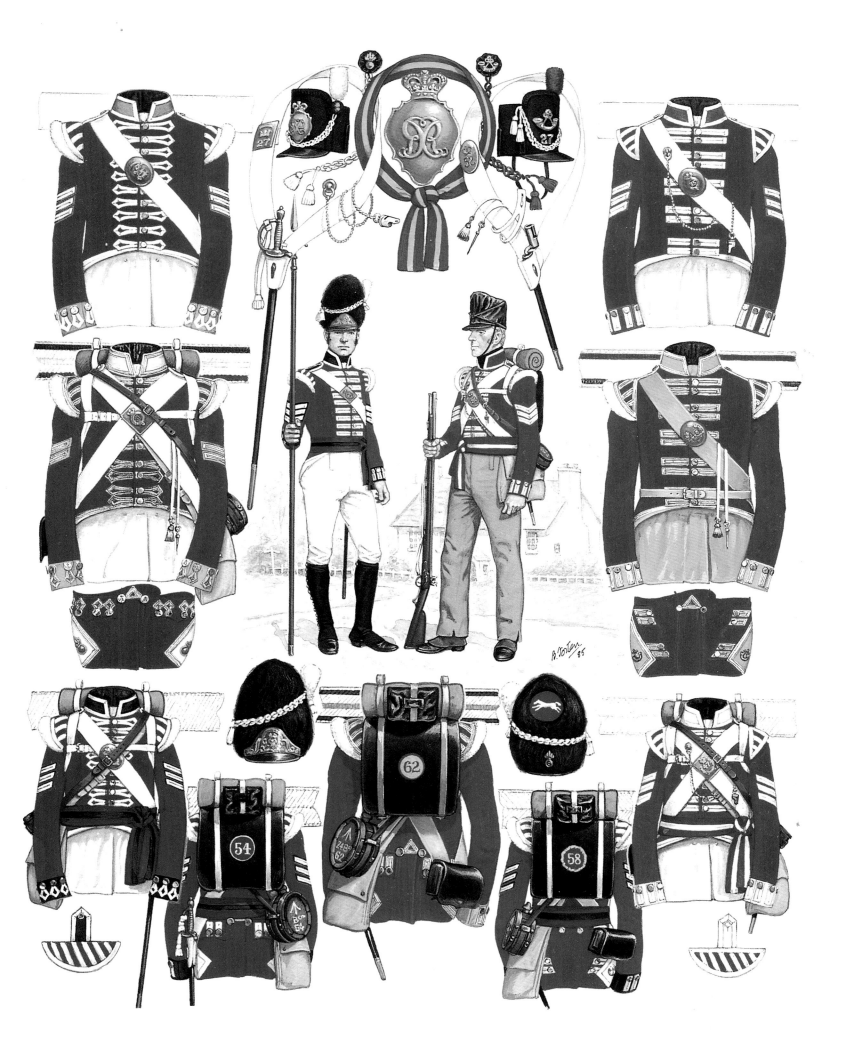

garlands, and white tufts on the left side. The rear of the cap had a red cloth patch bearing either the White Horse of Hanover or a special regimental device. For fatigue duty and daily camp wear the Other Ranks had forage caps. These were either of the flat-topped 'pork pie' shape, with a band in regimental facing colour and a top button; or of the folding, crescent-shaped pattern depicted in the Pyne sketches of campaign life.

Staff Sergeants and Sergeants had scarlet jackets with plain white silk or worsted lace. Corporals and Privates wore coarser, dull red jackets decorated with regimental lace – white worsted tape with interwoven coloured solid, broken or serpentine stripes to distinguish the regiment. Regiments with buff facings had buff jacket linings and turnbacks, the remainder, white. Officially, Grenadiers were to have horizontal pockets, Light Infantry sloping pockets and small buttons; in practice, these regulation distinctions seem largely to have been ignored. Both Flank Companies had red cloth shoulder wings, those of Grenadiers having six darts of lace and lace binding around the bottom edge, those of Light Infantry having six darts and binding all around. By 1815 most regiments had added drawn woollen thread tufting or thin worsted fringes to the outer edge of the wings.

Badges of rank were worn in the Flank Companies on both upper sleeves, and took the form of chevrons, each made of a doubled length of lace edged with regimental facing colour. Sergeants wore three plain white chevrons; Corporals, two chevrons of regimental lace. There was no central instruction regarding 'lance' appointments, but in some regiments men 'chosen' to be promoted were given a single chevron of regimental lace. An order of February 1813 authorised the rank of Colour Sergeant, for merit. Essentially fulfilling the functions of the later rank of Company Sergeant Major, these NCOs wore a distinctive 'honourable' badge on the right sleeve: a single white chevron, below a Union Flag with crossed silver and gold swords over the staff, below a Crown, the flag and crown in coloured silks. In Flank Companies three white chevrons were worn on the left sleeve. All Sergeants were also distinguished by crimson worsted waist sashes with a central stripe in regimental facing colour, or white in regiments with red or purple facings.

Full dress for home service and at major overseas garrisons included white breeches worn with knee-length black woollen gaiters buttoned up the outside. On other occasions trousers were worn, over dark grey half-gaiters. Trousers were initially adopted for service on hot-weather stations, and were of white cloth. Later their use became almost universal on campaign, and they were made in various grey shades.

Sergeants of Light Infantry were armed with fusils and bayonets; Grenadier Sergeants, with swords and 9ft. crossbar pikes. The fusil was either the Land Series weapon with a 33in. barrel; or the weapon generally favoured for Other Ranks of Light Infantry, the Land Series musket with a browned 39in. barrel. The Grenadier Sergeants' sword was a coarser version of the 1786 pattern Officers' weapon. Equipment belts were generally 2⅛in. wide, of whitened 'buff' ('buffalo') leather; a brass plate of regimental design was worn on the bayonet belt at the mid-point of the chest where it crossed the pouch belt. The wooden-framed 'Trotter' knapsack, of black-painted proofed cloth, bore either the regimental number or some other special regimental device on the outer flap.

XI

1812-1815

Infantry of the Line : Battalion Companies: Non-Commissioned Officers and Privates

The shako ordered in 1811, and issued from spring 1812, has been described under Flank Companies. In Battalion Companies it was dressed with white worsted cords (garlands), white over red tufts, and cockades with regimental buttons. The high false fronts of the shakos were often supported by strong wire bent to shape around the upper edge, and covered by the ribbed black edging braid. A white version of this shako was produced for the use of regiments proceeding overseas to hot-weather stations.

Battalion Company jackets had cross (horizontal) pockets, and tufts of drawn woollen threads at the outer ends of the shoulder straps. They were lined with white cloth (or buff, in regiments with buff facings); and the front skirts were turned and sewn back, and faced with white or buff serge. The jackets had ten loops of lace on each front, with buttons on the right front and holes on the left, and were made to button over to the waist. The loops were 4in. long at the top, tapering gradually to 3in. at the waist, and were set on horizontally. Each loop was made of a double length of lace, folded at the outer end into either a square, pointed, or 'bastion' shape.

The cuffs, collars and shoulder straps were in regimental facing colour. The collars were 3in. deep; like the shoulder straps, they were laced all round. The cuffs were 4½in. deep, and had four buttons and short loops of lace. Four buttons and lace loops were set on each pocket flap. Two buttons were set on the rear of the waist, on either side of a lace decoration which was ordered to be a diamond, but which in practice seems invariably to have been a triangle. The buttons on the cuffs, pocket flaps, and rear waist were larger than those on the other parts of the jacket. They were of pewter, bearing regimental numbers and/or designs, and were set on either spaced evenly, in pairs, or in threes, depending upon the regiment.

Sergeants had scarlet jackets, and plain white silk or worsted lace. Corporals and Privates had jackets of coarser red cloth, their white worsted lace interwoven with stripes and/or worms (serpentine or broken stripes) in various colours, distinguishing the regiment. Sergeant Majors had scarlet jackets of the double-breasted Officers' pattern, with gold or silver lace according to regimental practice.

Badges of rank were chevrons formed of doubled lengths of lace, each bar edged with cloth of the regimental facing colour, fixed half an inch apart on a piece of jacket cloth, and sewn to the upper right sleeve. Sergeant Majors wore four chevrons of gold or silver lace; Quartermaster Sergeants, four chevrons of plain white lace; Sergeants, three chevrons of plain white lace; Corporals, two chevrons of regimental lace. In regiments which distinguished Lance Corporals or Chosen Men, they wore one chevron of regimental lace. In 1813 the rank of Colour Sergeant was instituted as a recognition of

---

THE PLATE

Left side, top to bottom:
Jacket, epaulette and lace, Sergeant Major, 13th Regiment.
Jacket and lace, Colour Sergeant, 39th Regiment.
Jacket and lace, Sergeant, 14th Regiment, with full equipment.
Rank badge, Quartermaster Sergeant.

Centre, top to bottom:
1812 shako with Battalion Company distinctions; universal shako plate (without regimental distinctions); Sergeants' sash of a Royal Regiment; haversack and water canteen; cockade and garland for a Battalion Company.

Colour Sergeant, 39th Regiment, Service Dress.
Private, 18th Regiment, Service Dress.

Sergeants' sword hilt; rank badges of Sergeant Major and Sergeant; Privates' fatigue waistcoat of a Royal Regiment; Battalion Company fatigue cap of a yellow-faced regiment; two examples from among many differing types of regimental button design; Sergeants' pike head; Colour Sergeants' 'honourable badge'.

Right side, top to bottom:
Jacket, shoulder strap and lace, Corporal, 32nd Regiment.
Rear jacket details and lace, Private, 24th Regiment (the bayonet belt alone was worn when walking out).
Jacket and lace, Private, 59th Regiment, with full equipment.
Rank badges, Corporal; Lance Corporal or Chosen Man.

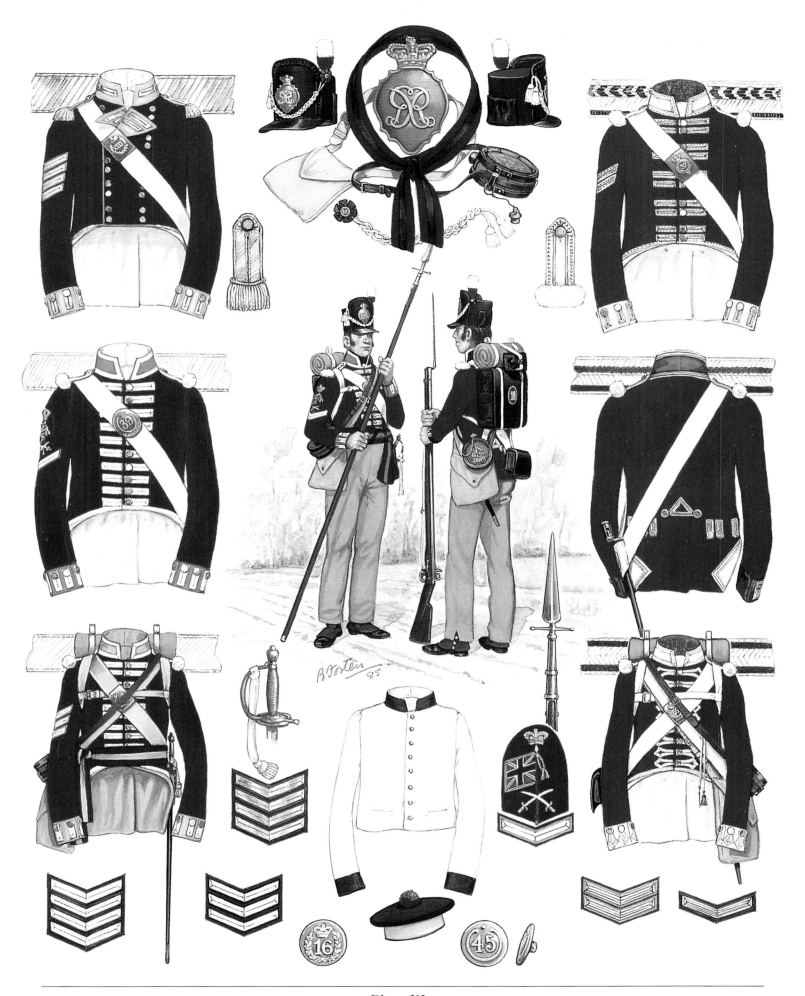

Plate XI 4

merit: the badge was a single white chevron, below a Union Flag surmounted by a Crown, both in coloured silks, with crossed silver, gold-hilted swords set over the flag staff.

Sergeants and senior NCOs were further distinguished by crimson worsted sashes with a central stripe in the regimental facing colour; those regiments whose facings were red or purple – the 33rd, 41st, 53rd, 56th and 76th Regiments – wore a white stripe. The sashes had no fringes; they were ordered to be knotted on the left hip, although contemporary illustrations indicate that they were tied on either side, and sometimes at the rear.

Official full dress included white breeches and knee-length black woollen gaiters. The breeches were made to come well up on the hips, and reached below the knee as far as the calf. Unlined except for the waist band, they had a pocket in the right side. The breeches had one small regimental button and white tape strings at each knee; and a second button at the rear just above each knee band, to keep up the gaiters. Sergeants had better quality breeches. Regiments with buff facings had breeches of the same colour. Over the previous decade trousers had been progressively adopted, originally for hot stations and for active service, but increasingly for all but ceremonial duties. Trousers of white 'Russia duck' were followed into use by various shades of grey or grey-blue, and during prolonged campaigning in the Peninsula much brown cloth was made up locally. Laced shoes or short ankle boots were worn with short dark grey cloth gaiters.

In 1812 it was ordered that Drummers and Fifers should henceforward wear jackets of the same colour as the rest of their regiments. However, British and French prints of the period up to and following Waterloo suggest that this order was often ignored, the jackets described by the 1802 Regulations continuing in use. These Regulations laid down that the coats of Drummers, Fifers, etc, of all Royal Regiments were to be of red, faced blue, with royal lace; and that for regiments whose facings were red the jackets were to be white with red facings. All other regiments were to use coats of the colours of their facings, faced red. All were to be lined white, except in regiments with white, red, black, or buff facings, which were to use red linings. The lace on the jackets was to be 'raised' above the common lace, and was a mixture of coloured worsted approaching the colours in the lace of the regimental rank and file. For ceremonial occasions Drummers and Fifers wore black bearskin caps, with brass plates bearing the Royal Crest with Trophies of Colours and Drums; but on all other occasions they wore shakos, in some cases with distinguishing tufts, e.g. reversed red over white.

Sergeant Majors were armed with swords of the 1786 Officers' pattern. Sergeants carried similar swords, and 9ft. crossbar pikes; for drills, and on other appropriate occasions, they carried canes. Corporals and Privates were armed with either the New Land or East India Pattern flintlock musket with a 42in. barrel; in Battalion Companies the barrels were not browned until after 1815. The musket slings were of white leather, and the bayonet scabbards were black. The shoulder belts supporting bayonet and cartridge pouch were of 2½in. buff leather, whitened with pipeclay except in buff faced regiments, which ochred the leather. A regimental belt plate ('breastplate') was fixed to the bayonet belt where it crossed the pouch belt on the chest. The plain black leather cartridge pouch carried 36 rounds.

XII

1815

Hussars, Waterloo Campaign

All four British Hussar Regiments fought in the Waterloo campaign of June 1815. The 7th, commanded by Sir Edward Kerrison, and the 15th, commanded by Leighton Dalrymple (although Captain Hancox assumed command during the engagement) were brigaded in Major General Sir Colquhoun Grant's Fifth Cavalry Brigade, together with the 2nd Hussars of the King's German Legion. Sir Hussey Vivian's Sixth Cavalry Brigade consisted of the 10th Hussars, commanded by Lt. Col. Quentin, and the 18th Hussars, commanded by Lt. Col. the Hon. Henry Murray, together with the 1st Hussars of the King's German Legion. Together, the four British regiments mustered approximately 68 Officers and 1,270 Other Ranks, plus the usual regimental staffs of Paymasters, Surgeons and Veterinaries.

In 1811 the facings of the 10th were changed from yellow to scarlet when the regiment became 'Royal'. The 10th, and the 7th – which had white facings – both received new clothing in 1814, with blue facings and gold or yellow lace. The 15th Hussars retained scarlet facings, and the 18th white facings, both with silver or white lace and buttons.

Three Hussar Regiments had worn shakos in the Peninsula, but the 7th and 15th discarded their outworn dark blue and scarlet shakos in favour of fur caps for the Waterloo campaign. Both regiments' caps had red bags, yellow cap lines and yellow metal chin scales. The 18th had worn fur caps during the whole period, and continued to do so, with bright blue bags, yellow lines and yellow metal chin scales. The 10th Hussars wore scarlet cloth-covered shakos. Dighton indicates a broad silver or white braid band around the upper edge; and the Officers had an additional row of gold interlocking rings, probably varying in size according to rank. Strangely, Dighton shows the 10th wearing their hair in queues both in the Peninsula and at Waterloo.

Clothing comprised laced jackets and laced, fur-trimmed pelisses, white leather or cloth pantaloons, and tasselled Hussar boots. Both Officers and Other Ranks had undress jackets made in simpler style, with less ornamentation. The rank and file had blue flannel stable jackets, which were worn with white duck trousers. Officers' Dress jackets and pelisses were made of fine cloth with very elaborate gold or silver lace and interlocking braid work, with complicated knots and braid figures up the sleeves. The regiments appear to have developed regimental styles of sleeve ornament. The 10th maintained its tradition of wearing a flat frame of braid around the frontal frogging.

The Officers' crimson silk cord sashes had gold, woven barrels, and were fitted with a slider, toggle, loop, and tasselled ends. They were wound around the waist approximately twice, and fastened with the toggle at the back, the long ends of the cords being brought around the right hip to fasten in front. Other Ranks of the 7th, 10th and 15th Hussars had dark red cord sashes with yellow barrels and details; the 18th had blue sashes with white fittings.

In the field, grey or dark blue overalls were worn. Officers of the 7th had silver stripes, the 10th

---

THE PLATE

Plate XII 12

and 18th a silver stripe, and the 15th scarlet stripes up the outward seams. The overalls were reinforced with black or tan leather strapping, and the Officers had fancy chains which fastened under the insteps. In Review Order, Hussars wore the jacket and had the pelisse slung over the left shoulder, retained by neck lines with flounders and tasselled ends. In winter the pelisse was worn in lieu of the jacket. For Levees and other special occasions Officers wore the jacket unfastened to reveal white, scarlet or blue waistcoats heavily laced and braided. The barrelled sash was worn over the waistcoat but under the jacket. Dighton shows the 10th and 18th of Vivian's Brigade charging at Waterloo; the 10th have their pelisses slung, but an Officer of the 18th appears to be wearing his.

Hussars were equipped with the pouch belt, pouch, waist sword belt with slings, and the sabretache. Officers' belts were faced with gold or silver lace, and their pouches and sabretaches were faced with elaborate regimental devices and badges. For Undress the belts were white, pouches and sabretaches black. Dighton shows an Officer of the 10th with a fawn cover over the sabretache, suggesting that the Dress item was worn in action. The rank and file had white 'buffalo' leather belts, the pouch belt fitted with a spring swivel for the carbine. Their pouches were plain black; and their plain black sabretaches were suspended by two slings, rather than the three used by Officers.

All ranks were armed with the 1796 Light Cavalry sabre; this had a broad, heavy, 33in. long curved blade, a steel knuckle bow guard, a black grip, and a steel backstrap with steel ears clamping the grip and rivetted on both sides. The scabbard was steel. The Officers' version of this weapon had a better quality blade and, being a private purchase, displayed occasional variations of detail from the regulation pattern. The Officers' sword knot was of gold and crimson silk, the Other Ranks' version of white leather. For Levees and special ceremonial occasions Officers were armed with sharply-curved and highly decorated 'Mameluke' sabres with crossbar hilts and ivory grips. Pistols were of the New Land Light Cavalry pattern, of .653in. calibre, with 9in. barrels. The carbines were of the so-called 'Paget' pattern, with 16in. barrels, swivel ramrods, V-shaped backsights and sloping foresights, and a steel bar on the left side to which the swivel hook could be clipped.

XIII

c1815

Light Dragoons

In 1812 there were fifteen regiments of Light Dragoons: the 8th, 9th, 11th, 12th, 13th, 14th, 16th, 17th, 19th, and 20th to 25th inclusive.

The 8th Light Dragoons had served under David Baird in Egypt in 1802, and subsequently went to India until 1822. The 9th had 86 years of uninterrupted service in Ireland before it came to England in 1803: the regiment later served in South America, the Netherlands and in the Peninsula until 1814. The 11th saw service in Egypt under Abercrombie; was in Germany in 1805; in Spain in 1811-1812; and fought at Waterloo. The 12th also served in Egypt, the Netherlands, in the Peninsula and at Waterloo. The 13th went to the Peninsula in 1810; it fought at Waterloo, and was subsequently posted to Paris. The 14th went out to Portugal with the first expedition in 1808; serving in Spain until 1814, the regiment was then sent to the West Indies, and thence to Louisiana, and was present at New Orleans. The 16th saw service both in the Peninsula and at Waterloo. The 17th, in Persia in 1810, subsequently served in India until 1823. The 19th – formerly numbered the 23rd – served in India, and later in Canada and America.

The 20th Light Dragoons served in Spain, in southern France, and also in Italy, including Naples. The 21st saw service in South Africa, sending detachments to Madeira as occupation troops. The 22nd – formerly the 25th, Gwyn's Hussars, until 1802 – served in the East Indies, and on the mainland during the Pindaree and Mahratta Wars. The 23rd – numbered the 26th until 1802 – fought in Spain and the Waterloo campaign under its new number. The 24th – until 1802, numbered the 27th – served alongside the 22nd in India. The 25th – formerly the 29th – served in India, Mauritius and the East Indies before its disbandment.

During the Waterloo campaign the 11th, 12th and 16th Light Dragoons formed the Fourth Brigade under Major General Sir John Vandeleur; the 13th, with the 3rd Hussars of the King's German Legion, formed Arendschildt's Seventh Brigade; and the 23rd served with the 1st and 2nd Light Dragoons of the King's German Legion as the Third Brigade, commanded by Major General Sir William Dornberg.

Between August and October 1811 new pattern clothing was approved for Light Dragoon Regiments. Instructions regarding Officers' uniforms were issued in December, and two Clothing Warrants followed in 1812.

Officers' shakos were of black felt with leather peaks, rear reinforcements and tops. They had bands of lace and braid front ornaments in gold or silver, gold or silver chin scales and matching holders for the feather plume. The cap lines were of gold and crimson mixed cord. Other Ranks had

---

THE PLATE

FIGURES:

Top left: *Officer, 9th Light Dragoons, Review Order; Officer, 13th Light Dragoons, campaign dress with pelisse, Spain.*
Centre: *Regimental Sergeant Major, 13th Light Dragoons, Review Order; Officer, 23rd Light Dragoons, Full Court Dress.*
Top right: *Sergeant, 12th Light Dragoons, Review Order; Corporal, 14th Light Dragoons, campaign dress, Spain.*
Bottom left: *Private, 16th Light Dragoons, campaign dress.*
Bottom right: *Private, 17th Light Dragoons, campaign dress, India.*

DETAILS:

Centre top: *Officers' girdle; Officers' sabretache, 14th Light Dragoons; Officers' pouch belt, 8th Light Dragoons; Officers' (hilt left) and Other Ranks' sabres, 1796 pattern; Officers' shako (left); Privates' shako.*
Left centre: *Brown and white versions of the shako, as worn in India and the Indies; Officers' (top) and Other Ranks' forage caps.*
Right centre: *Other Ranks' girdle (red facings, e.g. 16th Light Dragoons); Other Ranks' pouch and carbine belt, sword belt, sabretache, haversack and canteen.*
Centre bottom: *Officers' jacket, 17th Light Dragoons, with rear skirt details, and (above left) Lieutenant Colonels' epaulette of gold-laced regiments. Front and rear details of Other Ranks' jacket, 21st Light Dragoons, with (above right) Other Ranks' epaulette of silver-laced regiments.*

Plate XIII 14

similar shakos but with yellow or white ornaments, stubbier woollen plumes, yellow cap lines, and brass chin scales. Brown shakos were worn in the Indies, and a white pattern in India. Black oilskin covers were worn by all ranks in Marching Order.

Forage caps were blue. A French print shows gold or silver bands and top buttons for Officers. Other Ranks had similar caps with yellow or white bands. Contemporary paintings of Light Dragoons of the King's German Legion show Officers with brown fur caps with lace bands and tasselled tops.

Except for quality, the jackets of Officers and Other Ranks differed little. Officers' buttons were gilt or silver, Other Ranks' buttons pewter. Sources show varying numbers of buttons on the lapels, ranging from ten or seven down to as few as five. Officers' epaulettes, and the fringe or 'waterfall' in the rear waist of the jacket, were gold or silver, and those of Other Ranks yellow or white. Field Officers wore the usual badges of rank on their epaulette straps, in gold on silver or silver on gold. Regimental and Troop Sergeant Majors had four gold or silver chevrons, the former beneath a Crown; Sergeants had three chevrons, Corporals two and Lance Corporals one. Each bar of doubled lace was edged with the regimental facing colour, and all distinctions were worn on the right upper sleeve only.

In Review Order all ranks wore white breeches, or buff in the 9th, 11th and 13th Light Dragoons, with Hussar boots. For all other duties grey pantaloons or overalls were worn; Officers had Dress and Undress patterns, the former with two stripes of button-colour lace, the latter with two facing-colour stripes as worn by Other Ranks. Officers' girdles were gold with two crimson stripes. Other Ranks' were of facing colour with two blue stripes. Cloaks were blue with facing-colour collars. Officers' pelisses were similar to their jackets, with square-cut lapels and facing-colour linings. In Undress they might wear long pelisse coats, extravagantly frogged and braided.

In Watering Order the Other Ranks wore the forage cap and blue stable jacket. This had ten or twelve front buttons, and two at the rear of each pointed, facing-colour cuff; the blue collar had small yellow or white patches. White duck trousers were worn with this jacket.

From September 1811, Trumpeters were dressed similarly to the other Privates.

Officers' pouch and sword belts were faced with gold or silver lace, with a 'train' of the facing colour. Pouch belt fittings, including the pickers and chains, were silver. Sword belts had snake clasps. Dress sabretaches were faced with blue, and bore a universal design of gold lace edging, the Crown over 'GR' Cyphers and laurel sprays. Pouches were generally of leather, with a solid silver flap bearing a gilt Crown and Cypher. Other Ranks had broad white leather pouch belts and narrow sword belts (buff for the 9th, 11th and 13th). The pouch belt had brass fittings, and a steel spring swivel for the carbine; the sword belt had a snake clasp; and pouches and sabretaches were plain black leather.

All ranks were armed with 1796 pattern Light Cavalry pattern sabres in steel scabbards. Many Officers armed themselves with more flamboyant Mameluke-style sabres with ivory grips and decorated scabbards. Officers, senior NCOs and Trumpeters were also armed with the 1796 pattern pistol, and the other NCOs and Privates with the Paget carbine.

XIV

1815

Dragoons

In 1810. proposals were advanced that helmets should be provided to replace the old cocked hats worn by this branch. A decision on the design of this headdress was taken in March 1812. with the approval of the Prince Regent. However. the approved helmet – which had a brass peak, and was surmounted by a woollen crest – proved to be unsuitable. and it was not until August of that year that a final design was approved.

The metal parts of the new helmet were gilded for Officers and brass for Other Ranks. The leather peak was bound with metal. and the back of the leather skull was protected by rows of overlapping metal scales. An oval escutcheon superimposed on the front plate was inscribed with the title of the regiment. the front plate itself bearing the Royal Cypher. A long black horsetail was fixed along the top edge of the fluted metal crest. and normally hung to one side: it is sometimes depicted as partly plaited. or retained by ribbons. The chinstrap was covered with overlapping metal scales and suspended from rose bosses.

The 2nd Royal North British Dragoons. the Scots Greys. wore grenadier caps of black bearskin with gilded or brass front plates. gold or yellow cap lines. and a white feather plume on the left side. The red cloth rear patch bore the White Horse of Hanover: Officers' caps had. in addition. a small Thistle Star in white metal fixed into the fur below the rear patch. James Howe's painting of the regiment in bivouac before Waterloo shows the bearskin caps in black covers and without plumes. Hamilton Smith shows black covers for the Dragoon helmets.

Dragoon forage caps were blue for Other Ranks. and either blue with a fur trim, or all fur. for Officers. The cap band was of lace colour for Other Ranks. and of metallic lace for Officers. in regimental patterns. However. the Howe painting of the Scots Greys shows a red band with traditional white zig-zagging. and a red tourie. Heaphy also shows a tourie: Hamilton Smith does not. Officers had either a gold or silver top button. or a button and tassel.

The jackets were of the pattern approved in August 1812. replacing those worn since the beginning of the century: these had been single-breasted. with buttons. lace loops. and wings. The new jackets were also single-breasted. but closed down the front with hooks and eyes. They had broad lace down both fronts. along the edges of the turnbacks. and edging the pointed cuffs. Collars. cuffs and turnbacks were in facing colours. Officers' lace was gold or silver. with scalloped edges. and a central 'train' of the facing colour. Other Ranks' lace was of yellow or white worsted with a central stripe of facing colour. S. M. Milne and P. W. Reynolds confirm that this stripe was a feature of Dragoon lace.

THE PLATE

FIGURES:

Top left: Troop Sergeant Major. 1st (Royal) Dragoons. Service Dress: Sergeant. 2nd (Royal North British) Dragoons. Service Dress.

Centre: Regimental Sergeant Major. 6th (Inniskilling) Dragoons. Dress: Officer. 1st (Royal) Dragoons. Dress. with cocked hat.

Top right: Corporal. 3rd (King's Own) Dragoons. Parade Dress: Officer. 4th (Queen's Own) Dragoons. Dress.

Bottom left: Private. 6th (Inniskilling) Dragoons. Stable Dress.

Bottom right: Lance Corporal. 4th (Queen's Own) Dragoons. Walking-Out Dress.

DETAILS:

Centre top: Officers' helmet (front): Other Ranks' helmet (rear): Officers' Dress sabretache. 6th (Inniskilling) Dragoons: Officers' sword (hilt left) and 1796 pattern disc-hilted sword: Officers' girdle with tasselled ends: Officers' pouch belt and pouch.

Left centre: Officers' bearskin. 2nd (Royal North British) Dragoons. front and rear: Other Ranks' bearskin in oilskin cover: Other Ranks' forage cap. 2nd (Royal North British) Dragoons: Dragoon Other Ranks' forage cap. of yellow-laced regiment.

Right centre: helmet in waterproof cover: Other Ranks' sword belt. sabretache and pouch belt: Officers' forage cap.

Centre bottom: Officers' jacket. 2nd (Royal North British) Dragoons. with lace. rosette and shoulder cord detail: Other Ranks' jacket. 4th (Queen's Own) Dragoons. with lace and shoulder strap detail.

merit; the badge was a single white chevron, below a Union Flag surmounted by a Crown, both in coloured silks, with crossed silver, gold-hilted swords set over the flag staff.

Sergeants and senior NCOs were further distinguished by crimson worsted sashes with a central stripe in the regimental facing colour; those regiments whose facings were red or purple – the 33rd, 41st, 53rd, 56th and 76th Regiments – wore a white stripe. The sashes had no fringes; they were ordered to be knotted on the left hip, although contemporary illustrations indicate that they were tied on either side, and sometimes at the rear.

Official full dress included white breeches and knee-length black woollen gaiters. The breeches were made to come well up on the hips, and reached below the knee as far as the calf. Unlined except for the waist band, they had a pocket in the right side. The breeches had one small regimental button and white tape strings at each knee; and a second button at the rear just above each knee band, to keep up the gaiters. Sergeants had better quality breeches. Regiments with buff facings had breeches of the same colour. Over the previous decade trousers had been progressively adopted, originally for hot stations and for active service, but increasingly for all but ceremonial duties. Trousers of white 'Russia duck' were followed into use by various shades of grey or grey-blue, and during prolonged campaigning in the Peninsula much brown cloth was made up locally. Laced shoes or short ankle boots were worn with short dark grey cloth gaiters.

In 1812 it was ordered that Drummers and Fifers should henceforward wear jackets of the same colour as the rest of their regiments. However, British and French prints of the period up to and following Waterloo suggest that this order was often ignored, the jackets described by the 1802 Regulations continuing in use. These Regulations laid down that the coats of Drummers, Fifers, etc, of all Royal Regiments were to be of red, faced blue, with royal lace; and that for regiments whose facings were red the jackets were to be white with red facings. All other regiments were to use coats of the colours of their facings, faced red. All were to be lined white, except in regiments with white, red, black, or buff facings, which were to use red linings. The lace on the jackets was to be 'raised' above the common lace, and was a mixture of coloured worsted approaching the colours in the lace of the regimental rank and file. For ceremonial occasions Drummers and Fifers wore black bearskin caps, with brass plates bearing the Royal Crest with Trophies of Colours and Drums; but on all other occasions they wore shakos, in some cases with distinguishing tufts, e.g. reversed red over white.

Sergeant Majors were armed with swords of the 1786 Officers' pattern. Sergeants carried similar swords, and 9ft. crossbar pikes; for drills, and on other appropriate occasions, they carried canes. Corporals and Privates were armed with either the New Land or East India Pattern flintlock musket with a 42in. barrel; in Battalion Companies the barrels were not browned until after 1815. The musket slings were of white leather, and the bayonet scabbards were black. The shoulder belts supporting bayonet and cartridge pouch were of 2½in. buff leather, whitened with pipeclay except in buff faced regiments, which ochred the leather. A regimental belt plate ('breastplate') was fixed to the bayonet belt where it crossed the pouch belt on the chest. The plain black leather cartridge pouch carried 36 rounds.

XII

1815

Hussars, Waterloo Campaign

All four British Hussar Regiments fought in the Waterloo campaign of June 1815. The 7th, commanded by Sir Edward Kerrison, and the 15th, commanded by Leighton Dalrymple (although Captain Hancox assumed command during the engagement) were brigaded in Major General Sir Colquhoun Grant's Fifth Cavalry Brigade, together with the 2nd Hussars of the King's German Legion. Sir Hussey Vivian's Sixth Cavalry Brigade consisted of the 10th Hussars, commanded by Lt. Col. Quentin, and the 18th Hussars, commanded by Lt. Col. the Hon. Henry Murray, together with the 1st Hussars of the King's German Legion. Together, the four British regiments mustered approximately 68 Officers and 1,270 Other Ranks, plus the usual regimental staffs of Paymasters, Surgeons and Veterinaries.

In 1811 the facings of the 10th were changed from yellow to scarlet when the regiment became 'Royal'. The 10th, and the 7th – which had white facings – both received new clothing in 1814, with blue facings and gold or yellow lace. The 15th Hussars retained scarlet facings, and the 18th white facings, both with silver or white lace and buttons.

Three Hussar Regiments had worn shakos in the Peninsula, but the 7th and 15th discarded their outworn dark blue and scarlet shakos in favour of fur caps for the Waterloo campaign. Both regiments' caps had red bags, yellow cap lines and yellow metal chin scales. The 18th had worn fur caps during the whole period, and continued to do so, with bright blue bags, yellow lines and yellow metal chin scales. The 10th Hussars wore scarlet cloth-covered shakos. Dighton indicates a broad silver or white braid band around the upper edge; and the Officers had an additional row of gold interlocking rings, probably varying in size according to rank. Strangely, Dighton shows the 10th wearing their hair in queues both in the Peninsula and at Waterloo.

Clothing comprised laced jackets and laced, fur-trimmed pelisses, white leather or cloth pantaloons, and tasselled Husssar boots. Both Officers and Other Ranks had undress jackets made in simpler style, with less ornamentation. The rank and file had blue flannel stable jackets, which were worn with white duck trousers. Officers' Dress jackets and pelisses were made of fine cloth with very elaborate gold or silver lace and interlocking braid work, with complicated knots and braid figures up the sleeves. The regiments appear to have developed regimental styles of sleeve ornament. The 10th maintained its tradition of wearing a flat frame of braid around the frontal frogging.

The Officers' crimson silk cord sashes had gold, woven barrels, and were fitted with a slider, toggle, loop, and tasselled ends. They were wound around the waist approximately twice, and fastened with the toggle at the back, the long ends of the cords being brought around the right hip to fasten in front. Other Ranks of the 7th, 10th and 15th Hussars had dark red cord sashes with yellow barrels and details; the 18th had blue sashes with white fittings.

In the field, grey or dark blue overalls were worn. Officers of the 7th had silver stripes, the 10th

---

THE PLATE

FIGURES:

Top left: *Private and Officer, 10th Hussars.*
Centre: *Officer, 7th Hussars; Officer, 18th Hussars.*
Top right: *Sergeant and Private, 7th Hussars.*
Bottom left: *Officer and Private, 15th Hussars.*
Bottom right: *Sergeant Major and Private, 18th Hussars.*

DETAILS:

Centre top: *Officers' barrelled sash; Officers' sabretache, 15th Hussars; Officers' pouch belt, 7th Hussars; Officers' (hilt left) and Other Ranks' sabres; Officers' fur cap, 18th Hussars; Privates' shako, 10th Hussars.*
Left centre: *Privates' pelisse, 18th Hussars.*
Right centre: *Privates' barrelled sash, carbine and pouch belt, sabretache and sword belt.*
Centre bottom: *Front, rear and lace detail, Officers' jacket, 7th Hussars; front, rear and lace detail, Privates' jacket, 7th Hussars.*

Plate XI

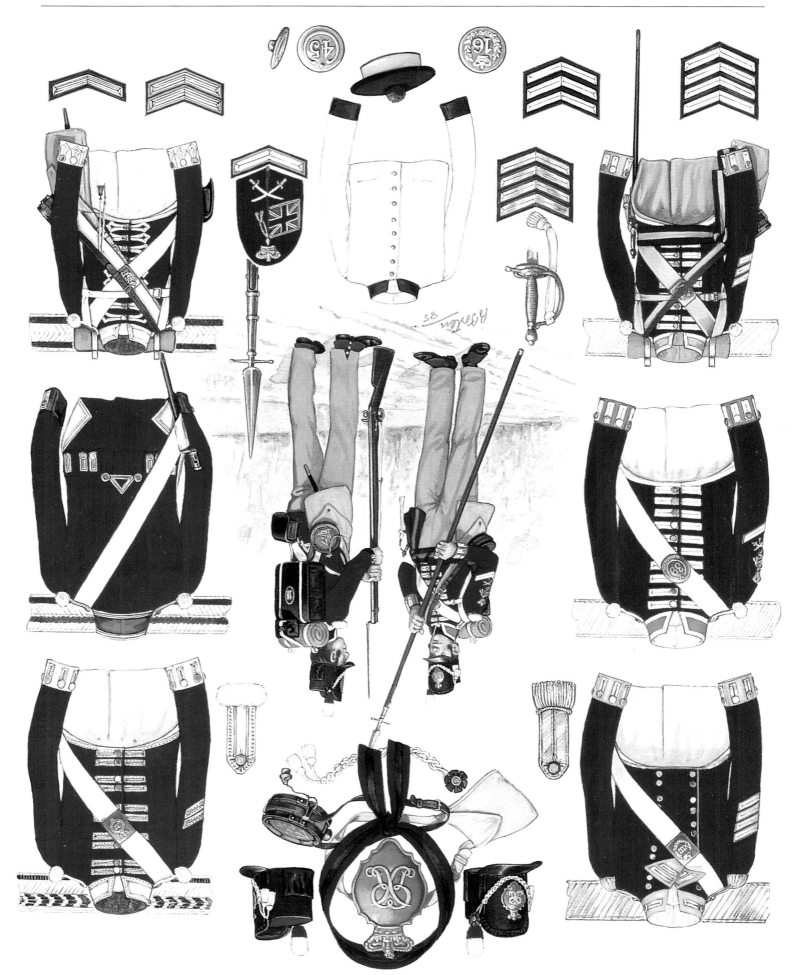

Plate XIV 18

and that Dragoon Guards' lace had a train pattern similar to that in the Officers' lace. Officers had narrow gold or silver twisted shoulder cords; Other Ranks had a length of regimental lace sewn to cloth backing. At the junction of turnbacks Officers wore a rosette of lace with a uniform button or some other regimental device sewn centrally; Other Ranks wore a button only.

For Undress, Officers wore an ankle-length blue frock or pelisse-coat elaborately decorated with black braid on the fronts, cuffs, collar, back seams and hips. The stable jackets of NCOs and Privates were red, with rectangular patches of the facing colour on the collars, pointed facing-colour cuffs, and ten pewter front buttons. Howe shows the Scots Greys wearing white jackets.

Officers had two forms of girdle, one fastened with toggles and loops on the left hip, the other with tasselled ends. For Undress they favoured a crimson silk sash knotted on the right hip. NCOs and Privates had webbing girdles in lace colour, with facing-colour stripes; regiments with yellow or white facings had either blue or red stripes.

Leather breeches and jackboots were reserved for parades. On other occasions Officers wore grey pantaloons with gold or silver stripes; for Undress and on campaign, grey pantaloons were reinforced with tan leather and decorated with red or facing-colour stripes. Other Ranks wore grey overalls strapped and cuffed with leather and with single or double red or facing-colour stripes, some with pewter buttons down the outward closure.

For Dress, Officers wore short white gloves. On active service all ranks wore white gauntlets, although Dighton shows the Greys with short gloves at Waterloo.

Officers' Dress belts were decorated with regimental lace; for Undress and on active service they had white belts. Dress pouches and sabretaches were faced with cloth, edged with regimental lace, and decorated with the Crown, Cypher and laurel sprays, in some cases with additional scrolls and regimental badges. Undress pouches and sabretaches were of black leather.

Officers were armed either with the 1796 Heavy Cavalry sword with a steel disc guard, as carried by Other Ranks, or with a similar straight-bladed sword with a pierced steel guard and silver wire-bound grip, both carried in steel scabbards. They also had a lighter Dress sword with a gilt pommel, knuckle bow and boat shells, a silver wire grip, and a black leather scabbard with gilt mounts. Officers' Dress knots were gold and crimson, Undress knots white leather with gold tassels; on campaign all ranks wore white leather knots. The 1796 pattern Heavy Cavalry carbine had a 26in. barrel, brass furniture, and a steel sling bar and ring. The 1802 pattern pistol had a swivel ramrod and brass furniture.

XV

1815

Dragoon Guards

In 1746 three regiments of Horse were converted to Dragoon Guards; and in 1788 a further four regiments were similarly redesignated, the seven regiments being numbered 1st to 7th in their new style.

A new helmet was proposed to replace the cocked hat in March 1812. This headdress, which had a brass peak and a thick, laterally-striped black and red woollen crest, proved unsatisfactory when issued to some units on trial, and in August 1812 it was replaced by a modified version resembling Dragoon headdress, with a long black horsetail *crinière*. A French print, after St. Fal, shows a Dragoon Guards Officer wearing this helmet in 1815 or 1816; a pair of black ribbons are shown flying loose from the horsetail. Another French print, from a series published in Paris in 1816, mentions that the horsetail, although fixed along the length of the metal crest, was confined with ribbons, only floating free from the lowest part; the illustration shows a series of small bows or ties along the upper edge of the comb. P. W. Reynolds recorded in his MS notes seeing a helmet in a private collection which had two black ribbons attached to the crest which could be tied round the middle of the horsetail. Other Ranks had a new helmet issued every three years.

Forage caps were blue, with a band of lace or facing colour, for Other Ranks. Both Finart and Howe show Privates with red touries to these caps; Hamilton Smith does not. Officers' caps were either of blue cloth with a lace band and fur lower trim; or all fur, with a lace band. They had a lace-coloured top button, with or without a pendant tassel. (A watercolour drawing, in the S. M. Milne collection, attributed to Eldridge, showed an Officer of the 5th Dragoon Guards wearing quite a large flat-topped fur cap with a lace-coloured band, a gold top button and a gold pendant tassel. He wore the jacket, girdle, and grey overalls with pale brown strapping and red piping or stripes.)

The jacket, approved in August 1812, closely resembled the Dragoon pattern. However, for Dragoon Guards the lace had a distinctive broken 'train' or 'worm' of facing colour; and the cuffs were of gauntlet shape, rather than pointed. In Buckmaster's old Tailor's Book there is an entry for an Officer's jacket of the 1st (King's) Dragoon Guards for 1815 or 1816:

'A Scarlet Jacket, single breasted, with blue velvet cuffs, collar and turnbacks, laced gold from top of the collar, down the fronts and edging the turnbacks. Lace to begin square at the hips. A piece of lace across the bottom. Stars for skirt ornaments. Cuffs cut to form a point at the hind arms (points to be

---

THE PLATE

Plate XV 23

loose) with a cord button under it. A piece of Royal Cord on a piece of the lace made to button or hook at the neck seam to retain the [pouch] belt. Fifteen large hooks and eyes in breast. 9 eyes and 6 hooks on the left and 9 hooks and 6 eyes on the right, all in 3s. Faced down inside of breast with scarlet. Lace 2¼in. wide.'

Hamilton Smith, who is said to have been working from sealed paterns, adds distinctive red collar patches for NCOs and Privates. A water-colour by J. A. Langendyck in Her Majesty the Queen's Collection at Windsor also shows this distinction; and it appears in another watercolour in the same collection, by Krausz. Other paintings in the Collection show Dragoon Guards with, or without, these patches. It seems that the red patches were not worn by Officers, and that their use by Other Ranks was abandoned in due course, but at an unspecified date.

In Hamilton Smith's series is a plate of Heavy Cavalry in foul weather dress. The helmet is shown in the black waterproof cover. The man wears a voluminous scarlet cloak without sleeves, with a short cape, a standing/falling collar of facing colour, and scarlet lining with a white facing down the fronts.

Officers wore two forms of girdle: one fastened with toggles and loops, the other tied with tasselled ends; they also had crimson silk sashes for undress. Other Ranks had web girdles in yellow or white, following regimental lace colour, with two stripes of facing-colour; these were blue-black for regiments with white or yellow facings. White breeches and high-topped boots were reserved for Review Order. On other Dress occasions Officers wore grey pantaloons with gold or silver stripes. On Field Days and on active service grey overalls were worn, with leather strapping and with red or facing-colour stripes. For all orders of dress other than Review, Other Ranks wore grey overalls strapped with leather, with red or facing-colour stripes, and in some cases with pewter buttons down the outside closure.

For Dress, Officers wore short white gloves, but on active service all ranks wore gauntlets. Officers' Dress pouch and sword belts were faced with regimental lace; for Undress, and on active service, white belts were worn. Embroidered pouches and sabretaches were similarly worn for Dress, and black leather pouches and sabretaches on all other occasions. Other Ranks had white carbine belts with buckled straps for the black pouches, carbine swivel loops, white sword belts and slings, and black sabretaches.

Officers and Other Ranks were armed with the 1796 pattern steel disc-hilted sword. Some Officers acquired swords with pierced steel guards and silver wire grips; and for Dress or Undress they carried lighter weapons, with gilt pommels, boat shells, knuckle bow guards, wire grips, and gilt-mounted black scabbards. Sword knots were white, with gold tassels for Officers; the latter also had gold and crimson knots for some Dress and Undress occasions. The 1796 cavalry carbine carried by Other Ranks had a 26in. barrel, brass furniture, and a steel swivel bar with sliding ring.

XVI

1812-1815

Royal Regiment of Artillery

The Royal Artillery did not come under the control of 'Horse Guards': it was controlled by the Master General of the Ordnance. and as such was not dealt with as part of the Army when Warrants and Regulations were issued. Its Officers were promoted by seniority and upon merit. and not by purchase.

Duncan's *History* of the Regiment gives the strength of the Royal Artillery at Waterloo. 1815. as 25 Officers and 475 NCOs and Privates. with 30 guns. Other companies were also detached to deal with the Field Park. and to man the Siege Train then in the process of assembly at Ostend and Antwerp. The Corps of Drivers comprised seven Officers and 6.000 NCOs and Privates. this imbalance possibly due to the dispersion of Drivers on campaign under the authority of the Royal Artillery Officers of the companies to which they were attached.

By August 1813. Board of Ordnance General Orders confirm that the Royal Artillery had taken into use the high-fronted shako approved for the Infantry in March 1812. The Orders stated: 'The cocked hat worn by Staff Sergents and the cap of sugar loaf shape [the cylindrical 1802 shako] worn by other NCOs and men is discontinued. A cap of low crown and false stand up collar [sic] of the Belgian fashion with cord and tassel [is to be] worn by Officers and men . . .'

Officers retained the use of the cocked hat for Levees. Drawing Rooms and Dining Out occasions. Officers' shakos had gold and crimson festoons and tassels and white cut-feather hackles. NCOs and Privates had yellow worsted cords and tassels and white woollen tufts: one contemporary source gives white cords. Black oiled cloth covers were worn in bad weather and in the field. The shako plates were of a similar shape to those used by the Infantry. and were surmounted by Crowns. The Officers' gilt plate bore the three Ordnance Guns and Balls: Other Ranks had brass plates with a Garter inscribed 'ROYAL REGIMENT OF ARTILLERY' enclosing the Royal Cypher: beneath the Garter was a mortar flanked by two flaming bombs.

Officers had dark blue. long-tailed. gold-laced Dress coats with scarlet facings. plain unlaced coats for everyday use. and shorter-tailed laced jackets. The buttons were gilded. and the gold lace loops were point-ended and set at equal distances. Officers' turnbacks were probably white on the Dress coats and scarlet for the plain coat and jacket. Other Ranks wore jackets similar in cut and style to the Infantry coat of the period. with red facings. and yellow bastion-ended loops at equal distances: their buttons were pewter. Hamilton-Smith shows red turnbacks for 1812: Dighton shows white pre-1812 but red for 1815. Staff Sergeants and Sergeants had gold lace.

Field Officers had two bullion epaulettes with gold lace straps and silver rank badges in the usual sequence. Captains and Subalterns wore one epaulette on the right shoulder. the former with bullions. the latter with a thinner fringe. Staff Sergeants wore four and Sergeants three gold lace chevrons on

---

THE PLATE

Plate XVI 19

both upper sleeves. Company Sergeants – the equivalent of Colour Sergeants of Infantry – wore the Colour Badge above one gold chevron on the right sleeve. and three gold chevrons on the left. Corporals wore two and Bombardiers one yellow worsted chevron on both upper sleeves. All badges were sewn on red backing cloth. Officers had crimson silk net and senior NCOs crimson worsted sashes knotted at the left hip.

For Dress occasion Officers wore white pantaloons with either knee-length boots. cut away behind the knee. or Hessians. NCOs and Privates wore white breeches and knee-length black woollen gaiters with horn buttons for Dress parades: but Atkinson and a contemporary French print show blue pantaloons with yellow or gold stripes up the outward seams. probably a Walking-Out dress. In the field and for everyday use all ranks wore grey trousers over short dark grey gaiters: Officers were also permitted dark blue pantaloons. Dighton shows gunners with white duck overalls with black buttons.

Officers were armed with swords similar to the 1786 pattern used by the Infantry. Mounted Field Officers were armed with similar weapons or with more ornate sabres. including Mameluke styles. from slings on a waist belt. Staff Sergeants had brass-mounted versions of the Officers' sword: Company Sergeants and Sergeants were armed with 9ft. crossbar pikes. and short. brass-hilted hangers. Corporals and Privates were armed with the Artillery carbine and bayonet. although Hamilton-Smith shows two gunners with hangers. Belts were of white leather. Officers and Staff Sergeants had gilded or brass belt plates. but junior ranks seem to have had only brass buckles on the hanger/bayonet belts. Corporals and Privates were equipped with small white leather cartridge pouches with brass labelled Crown badges on the flap. mounted on red cloth. On the front of the pouch belt were runners retaining brass priming tools. and smaller runners keeping a red flask cord: the horn flask, with brass nozzle and mounts, rested on the pouch flap. Hamilton-Smith shows no tools on the belts, and it seems likely that only selected men would have been issued with them.

XVII

1816-1820

9th Light Dragoons (Lancers)

Wynne's Dragoons were raised in 1715. After seeing action in minor skirmishes during the Jacobite Rebellion the regiment went out to Ireland. In 1783 it was converted to a Light Dragoon regiment. It served in Ireland during the 1798 Rebellion. and fought at Vinegar Hill. After some 86 years of uninterrupted service in Ireland the regiment returned to England in 1803. It was then still partly uniformed as a Dragoon regiment. and had to be totally re-clothed and equipped as a Light Dragoon unit.

In 1809 the 9th Light Dragoons went to the Low Countries. fighting at Walcheren and taking part in the siege of Flushing. In 1806 it was shipped to South Africa; and from the Cape to South America. where it took part in the disastrous campaign which culminated in the abortive attack on Buenos Aires. fighting as infantry. Returning to the United Kingdom much reduced. the 9th recruited up to strength before going out to the Peninsula. The regiment served in Portugal and Spain until 1814. when it returned to Britain. where it remained until 1816.

In September 1816 it was decided to equip four Light Dragoon Regiments as Lancers. Alterations in the uniform took place towards the end of 1817. The four regiments chosen were the 9th. 12th. 16th and 23rd. The last-named was disbanded in 1817. however. being replaced by the 19th: and. when that regiment was also disbanded. by the 17th Light Dragoons. on their return from India in 1822.

The headdress chosen for the newly equipped regiments was the 'schapska' – the Polish-style cap already in use by many European lancer regiments. It had a 10in. square top. a front and back peak. scalloped chin scales. and a drooping plume from a socket behind a large rosette on the left front. The Officers' caps were trimmed with gold and crimson cord: they had much gold lace. a large front plate. and gilded chin scales. The plume was a large white-over-crimson cock's tail: and the elaborate gold cap lines had flounders. olivets and tassels. Officers also had a simpler Undress cap without a front plate and with a horsehair plume. NCOs and Privates had simpler caps of the same style. with yellow cords. worsted lace. a brass plate and chin scales. and a white and crimson horsehair plume. Their Undress caps were blue with a facing-colour band.

The dark blue jackets were similar to the Light Dragoon pattern. but the Officers' had gold embroidered loops on the ends of the collars and embroidered edging to the cuffs. The coats had two gold bullion back pieces with embroidered heads at the back of the waist. but regulations make no mention of slashed pockets. as they do for the Light Dragoons. The small skirts had crimson turnbacks. and the back and sleeve seams were welted with crimson. Each narrow crimson lapel had nine gilt buttons with one at the top. and the fronts were closed with hooks and eyes. NCOs and Privates had jackets of similar pattern. Sergeants having gold lace collar loops and cuff edging and Privates having yellow lace. Note that Dighton and Alken show Other Ranks with round rather than pointed cuffs for this period. All jackets were made so that the lapels could be buttoned back. displaying the crimson facings. or buttoned over showing the blue side.

THE PLATE

FIGURES

Top left and right: *Sergeant and Private.*
Centre. left to right:
Officer. Full Dress; Officer. Mixed Dress; Corporal.
Bottom left: *Officer. Undress.*
Bottom right: *Officer in overcoat and Undress cap.*

DETAILS

Top centre: *Officers' lance cap, front and rear; Officers' sabretache. set over Other Ranks' sabre (hilt left) and Officer's dress sabre; Officers' pouch belt. pouch and girdle.*
Centre left: *Officers' Undress sabretache.*
Centre right: *Officers' epaulettes with badges for Lieutenant Colonel and Major. above Other Ranks' brass epaulettes.*
Bottom centre: *Officers' jacket. closed as for Marching Order. with skirt tassel details. and cap lines (left); Privates' jacket. closed as for Marching Order. with cap lines.*

Plate XVII 26

Officers had gold aiguillettes fixed at the right shoulder and looped across the breast to fasten to a button of the lapel. They also had two large bullion epaulettes with crimson straps richly embroidered with gold. Field Officers had silver rank badges, in the usual sequence. Other Ranks had stout brass scale epaulettes. The Regimental Sergeant Major's badge was four chevrons with a Crown above; Troop Sergeant Majors had a four-bar chevron, and Sergeants three. Sergeants and senior NCOs had gold lace chevrons. Corporals two chevrons of yellow worsted.

Officers' crimson Dress trousers were in the full-hipped, tapered, 'Cossack' style, with 1¾in. wide gold lace stripes; they also had a grey pattern with similar gold stripes, worn in a mixed dress. Their Undress trousers were blue-grey with two ¾in. wide crimson stripes. Other Ranks had grey trousers with single crimson stripes.

Officers' Undress jackets resembled the stable jackets worn in subsequent periods. The jackets had no tails, were closed with many gilt studs, and were edged with gold lace: 1½in. wide for Field Officers, 1in. for Captains, and ¾in. for Subalterns. Other Ranks had blue stable jackets.

Officers' girdles were gold with two crimson stripes; Other Ranks had yellow worsted girdles with two red stripes. Officers' Dress sword and pouch belts were faced with gold lace, with crimson stripes; pickers, chains and fittings were silver, and the pouch flaps were silver with gilt ornaments. Officers' Undress sword belts and sabretache was richly embroidered and edged with gold lace.

For Dress occasions Officers were armed with Mameluke-style sabres with ivory grips, gilt crossbar hilts, and crimson velvet scabbards with gilt mountings. Officially the Undress sword had a steel half-basket hilt with two bars and a polished steel scabbard; Dighton shows a Mameluke sabre carried in a steel scabbard.

Other Ranks had white leather belts; their sabretaches were of plain black leather and, as they did not carry carbines, the pouch belt had no spring swivel. They were armed with 1796 pattern steel-hilted sabres in steel scabbards, and 9ft. ash pole lances with red and white pennons.

XVIII

1825

71st Regiment of Foot (Highland Light Infantry)

The 71st Highland Light Infantry were raised as the 73rd Highlanders in 1777. Initially recruited in both the Highlands and Lowlands of Scotland, the regiment came in time to be associated with Glasgow, and particularly with the Paisley district. In 1779 the regiment embarked for India, where it fought with distinction under Sir Eyre Coote. A second battalion was raised, and served at the siege of Gibraltar, but subsequently returned home, to be disbanded in 1783. The 1st Battalion became the 71st (Highland) Regiment in 1786, and continued to serve in India until 1798. A second battalion was again raised in 1803.

The 1st Battalion was with Baird in South Africa in 1806; and was shipped to South America, suffering severely in the Buenos Aires expedition, which ended in the surrender of the British force. After repatriation the regiment went out to the Peninsula under Sir John Moore, returning home in 1809. It was then made a Light Infantry Regiment in recognition of its services; and was permitted to retain some elements of its Highland dress, provided that these did not interfere with its Light Infantry duties. The 1st Battalion served at Walcheren, in the Peninsula from 1810 to 1814, and at Waterloo. Between 1825 and 1832 the regiment – a single-battalion corps once more since 1815 – served in Canada.

There are early references to the 71st wearing a 'bonnet cocked of the approved pattern'. By 1810 Other Ranks had adopted as headdress the blue 'hummle' bonnet 'cocked' or set up in the shape of a low Light Infantry cap. It was provided with a detachable leather peak, secured with ribbons which were pendant at the back; and had a green Light Infantry tuft, a diced band, and a stringed bugle-horn badge. A French caricature of the period after Waterloo, when the regiment served in the Army of Occupation until 1818, shows a red top button or tourie and a yellow stringed bugle-horn badge. At this period Officers appear to have worn the conventional black felt Light Infantry shako without the diced band, but with a silver bugle-horn badge and a green feather.

A new pattern Infantry shako was approved in August 1816, and modified in 1822. Officers of the 71st had blue shakos 7½in. high in front and somewhat deeper at the back; the tops were approximately 10in. in diameter. The caps had black leather peaks, band of Thistle pattern braid around the top and bottom edges, silver bugle-horn badges, and, for ceremonial occasions, black cord cap lines. The shakos replaced cocked hats for Court attendances, Drawing Rooms, etc. A dark green ball ornament was used by the 71st in lieu of the more usual green feather or tuft. The cap did not have chin scales, but a leather strap was used for some orders of dress. Other Ranks wore caps of blocked blue bonnet cloth with woven diced bands, red touries, and black cap lines for parades. The Undress cap for all ranks was the blue 'hummle' bonnet with diced band, touries, and – for Officers – a small leather peak.

THE PLATE

FIGURES:

Top left: *Colour Sergeant, summer Review Order; Private, winter Review Order.*
Centre, left to right:
Sergeant Major; Paymaster; Major in Levee Dress.
Top right:
Company Officer, Review Order; Sergeant, winter Marching Order.
Bottom left: *Corporal, duties in cantonments.*
Bottom right: *Quartermaster Sergeant.*

DETAILS:

Top centre: *Officers' shako, Officers' forage cap, Other Ranks' shako; Officers' shoulder belt plate, set over Officers' sword (hilt left), Sergeants' sword, Officers' sash; Other Ranks' cockade ornament.*
Centre left: *Officers' and Other Ranks' buttons, Other Ranks' forage cap, Field Officers' epaulette and wing, Company Officers' wing, Officers' turnback ornament.*
Centre right: *Other Ranks' cross belt plate, Other Ranks' equipment, Sergeants' sash, Sergeants' sword and bayonet belt.*
Bottom centre: *Privates' jacket, with details of lace, shoulder strap and wing; (right) Company Officers' jacket; whistle detail.*

Plate XVIII 28

The Light Infantry wore short-tailed jackets until 1826. The coats had 3in. deep Prussian collars, 3in. deep round cuffs, 'cuirass'-shaped lapels, and, for the Officers, buttons in pairs (tailors' pattern books), white turnbacks and slashed pockets. Officers had silver bugle-horn turnback ornaments; and scarlet wings lined buff, reinforced with silver chains and with silver bullions and gold bugle-horn ornaments. Field Officers wore silver bullion epaulettes over their wings, with gold rank badges in the usual sequence and worn together with gold bugle-horns.

Senior NCOs and Sergeants had scarlet jackets, Corporals and Privates red. For all Other Ranks the looping was square-ended and set on at equal distances; the white regimental lace had a red stripe. The NCOs' badges of rank were: Sergeant Major, four silver chevrons, probably with Crown over; QM Sergeant, four white chevrons; Colour Sergeant, the Colour Badge on the right sleeve, three white chevrons on the left; Sergeant, three white chevrons; Corporal, two chevrons, and Lance Corporal, one chevron, of regimental lace. Chevrons were worn on both sleeves. All Other Ranks had wings, the Sergeant Major's silver, all others red, barred and edged with lace and with large drawn thread rolls on the outer edges.

Officers' trousers were blue-grey with ¾in. wide silver lace down the outward seams, edged on both sides with crimson. They wore white trousers in summer, and white pantaloons with Hessian boots at Levees. In Drawing Rooms, at Balls, etc., they wore white breeches, silk stockings and buckled shoes. Other Ranks wore white trousers in summer, and grey between October and March.

Officers had crimson silk sashes, worn Highland fashion over the left shoulder and knotted on the right hip. Senior NCOs had crimson worsted sashes with buff stripes, worn in the same way. Buglers wore red jackets with special regimental lace, including over all seams. The Paymaster, Quartermaster and Surgeons wore single-breasted jackets without wings, sashes or badges, and had cocked hats, the Paymaster's with a silver loop.

Officers' overcoats were dark blue, single-breasted, with Prussian collars; and they also had blue cloaks lined with red shalloon. Sergeants and senior NCOs had grey greatcoats like those of the men, but with buff collars and cuffs. Officers' buttons were small, silver, and bore a Crown and '71' in the curl of a French bugle; Other Ranks had pewter buttons with the same design. Officers and Other Ranks had silver and brass shoulder belt plates of similar design, as illustrated.

Officers were armed with 1822 pattern Infantry swords. Sergeants and Other Ranks were armed with New Land Service pattern Light Infantry muskets with browned 3ft. 3in. barrels. Sergeants were armed with muskets and swords, and had signal whistles on their belts.

(Thanks are extended to Messrs. W. Y. Carman and G. Gibbs for their help in preparing this plate.)

XIX

1853-1854

33rd Regiment of Foot

In 1852, following the death of the 1st Duke of Wellington. the Queen graciously directed that the 33rd (1st York. West Riding) Regiment. of which he had been Colonel from 1806 to 1813. should henceforth be known as the Duke of Wellington's Regiment. bearing his Crest and Motto in its appointments. It was (and remains) the only British Regiment to be named after a subject of the Crown.

The shako was the pattern authorised in 1844. For Officers it was of black beaver. with a gilt plate. chain. 'rose' pattern bosses and tuft socket. The ball tufts were white with the lower third red for Field and Battalion Company Officers; all-white for Grenadiers; and all-green for the Light Infantry Company. NCOs and Privates wore black felt shakos of similar design. with brass plates. tuft sockets. etc.. and black leather chin straps. Flank Company plates had smaller numerals in the centre of the plate. with a grenade or bugle-horn above. The Sergeant Major had an Officers' pattern shako with a star plate and chin chain.

The 33rd had red facings. Officers' coatees were scarlet and had two rows of gilt regimental buttons. ten in each row. set on in pairs; the rows were 3in. apart at the top and 2½in. apart at the bottom. The coatees had Prussian style collars. with two ¼in. wide gold lace loops. a small gilt button being set at the outer end of each. The plain round cuffs were 2¾in. deep. with scarlet slashed flaps up the sleeves bearing four short gold lace loops each set centrally with a small gilt button. In the rear of the waist were two large buttons; but by this date the slashed pocket flaps had been discontinued. The white kersey turnbacks had ornaments comprising gold embroidered eight-point stars set on scarlet backing cloth. with the White Rose of York in the centre.

Sergeants and senior NCOs also had scarlet double-breasted coatees. with pewter regimental buttons set on in pairs. Their red collars were edged with plain white lace. and bore single white lace 'bastion' loops. The scarlet cuff flaps bore three white lace loops with buttons. The coatees had white kersey turnbacks; NCOs of Flank Companies had brass grenade or bugle-horn ornaments. The Sergeant Major and Staff Sergeants had silver collar and cuff lace.

Corporals and Privates had red coatees of coarser material. Their collars and cuffs were of the same pattern as those of the Sergeants. but their coatees were single-breasted. with a single row of ten pewter regimental buttons set on in pairs. and 'bastion'-ended white lace loops on the fronts.

For Undress. Officers wore scarlet shell jackets with plain red Prussian collars and pointed cuffs.

THE PLATE

FIGURES

Top left: Sergeant Major, summer linen trousers; Officer, Light Infantry Company – note whistle on shoulder belt, and sash tassels carried to breast button.
Centre: The Colonel; the Adjutant, in forage cap and shell jacket.
Top right: Corporal, Battalion Company; Sergeant, Grenadier Company, field dress with greatcoat.
Bottom left: Light Infantry Company Private wearing transitional grey trousers which superceded the white linen summer pattern.
Bottom right: Bandsman in Review Order.

DETAILS

Centre top: Officers' (left) and Other Ranks' shakos (Battalion Company). tufts of Light Infantry (left) and Grenadier Companies, Officers' above Other Ranks' shako plates (Battalion Company); Officers' shoulder belt plate; Officers'

1882 pattern sword hilt; Officers' swords with brass, and gilt-mounted black leather scabbards, set over Officers' sash (Battalion and Grenadier Companies).
Centre left: Epaulettes of (left to right) Colonel, Captain, Sergeant Major; and Other Ranks' shoulder strap, Battalion Company; Grenadier Officers' wing. Flank Company Other Ranks' shoulder strap and wing; Light Infantry Company Officers' forage cap, Battalion Company Other Ranks' forage cap, Light Infantry Company Other Ranks' forage cap.
Centre right: Other Ranks' marching equipment showing knapsack with rolled blanket, mess tin in cover, cartridge pouch, waistbelt with Sergeants' skirling bayonet frog, percussion cap pouch, and expense pouch.
Bottom centre: Coatees of (left to right): Private, with collar, turnback, and button details – Long Service & Good Conduct chevron on right forearm; Sergeant, Battalion Company, with alternative Flank Company turnback ornaments in detail; Officer, with collar and button detail.

Plate XIX 10

The jackets were hooked close, but had a row of small gilt buttons set on in pairs, and two buttons on the rear of each cuff. On the shoulders were gold 'basket-weave' straps — interwoven cords — with trefoil 'figures' at the outward ends.

Field Officers' epaulettes had plain gold straps with silver-embroidered Royal Cyphers on the pads: Captains and Subalterns had gold straps striped with scarlet silk. Field Officers' badges of rank were worn on the straps in silver embroidery: a Crown and Star, a Crown, and a Star for Colonel, Lieutenant Colonel and Major respectively. Officers of Flank Companies wore wings, the straps and shells covered with gilt chain: Grenadiers had silver grenades. Light Infantry Officers silver bugle-horns, worked on the gilt centre plates.

The Sergeant Major and Staff Sergeants had silver-laced shoulder straps with silver metal crescents. Sergeants and junior ranks of Battalion Companies had straps of facing cloth edged with white lace, with large white worsted crescents, retained by narrow white bridles. Flank Company Other Ranks had similar straps, but with scarlet or red wings, barred and edged with plain white lace.

Non-Commissioned Officers' badges of rank were worn on the right upper sleeve by Staff Sergeants and Battalion Company NCOs, but on both sleeves in Flank Companies. The Sergeant major wore his four chevrons on the lower right sleeve beneath a Crown. The Sergeant Major and Staff Sergeants had silver chevrons, all other NCOs plain white chevrons. The Colour Sergeants had gold embroidered Crowns over Union Flags with crossed Roman swords on the staffs, above a single white chevron, on the right sleeve: Flank Company Colour Sergeants wore, in addition, three white chevrons on the left upper sleeve. Sergeants' greatcoats had red collars and cuffs, and the badges of rank were scarlet.

The Officer' forage cap worn with Undress had a small peak, a black silk oakleaf-pattern band, and gold embroidered badges. Staff Sergeants wore similar peaked caps: Sergeants and junior ranks wore dark blue knitted Kilmarnock caps with brass badges, the coloured tuft identifying the company – blue, white or green for Battalion, Grenadier or Light Infantry.

In 1829 'Oxford mixture' trousers, virtually black in colour, were taken into winter use between October and April. In 1833 a 1½in. scarlet stripe was added to the trousers of Officers, and a red ¼in. welt to those of Other Ranks. White linen trousers were worn during the summer months; but in 1845 these were replaced by grey or lavender-grey tweed trousers. By 1850 these fugitive dyes had proved unsuccessful, and were gradually replaced by indigo.

Officers were armed with the 1822 pattern sword with a gilded half-basket hilt with 'VR' set in the outward bars, and a black grip. The scabbard was brass for Field Officers: black with gilded mounts for all others, and for Field Officers in evening or Court Dress. Adjutants had steel scabbards in the field. Sword knots were crimson and gold with bullion tassels. Staff Sergeants' swords were of a similar pattern, with black, brass-mounted scabbards and white knots. Band and Drummers' swords were of regimental pattern.

Infantry Regiments proceeding to the Crimea were generally armed with the Minié Rifle, of .702in. calibre, a 3ft. 3in. barrel, and an overall length of 6ft. ½in. including fixed socket bayonet. The pouch belt was 2½in. wide, the black pouch approximately 7½in. long by 3½in. deep, holding 60 rounds. The 1850 pattern adjustable waistbelt was 2in. wide, and had a brass circular locket clasp with the regimental number and title. A brown leather cap pouch was worn on the right front, and in some cases a black leather expense pouch with reserve ammunition was worn on the front or rear. The bayonet frog was V-shaped and fixed for Corporals and Privates, and sliding for Sergeants. The knapsack was of black-painted canvas. Photographs show the haversack and canteen carried over the left shoulder to hang on the right hip; but several contemporary sketches executed in the Crimea show both items carried the reverse way.

1854

Light Dragoons

In 1844 the heavy and uncomfortable bell-shaped shako introduced in 1828 was replaced by a smaller and simpler headdress. The Officers' pattern was of black beaver, 7in. high at the front, 8in. high at the back, and 8in. in diameter across the top. It had a black patent leather peak sloping downwards at an angle, edged with 1in. gold embroidery. The black patent leather top surface was slightly sunken; and the upper edge was bound with gold oakleaf pattern lace 1¾in. wide. The shako plate, of the same pattern as worn on the previous model, comprised a large crowned silver and gilt Maltese Cross, with central regimental badges. The gilded brass chain had 'rose' bosses; and the gold cord cap lines, with 'olive' terminals, were worn twice round the shako, usually crossing at the back. The plume was of white swans' feathers, 5in. on the mount with 14in. long drooping outward feathers; in India white horsehair plumes of similar dimensions were substituted; the plume socket was gilt.

NCOs and Privates wore a headdress of very similar appearance, but made of black felt. Their caps had 1in. wide yellow worsted braid around the top edge; a brass crowned Maltese Cross plate; yellow cord cap lines; a brass chain; and a drooping white horsehair plume in a brass socket. In the field, black oiled silk or skin covers were worn, with the cap lines over them. On hot stations white quilted calico covers were worn, with detachable neck curtains, and similarly arranged cap lines.

The dark blue jackets were double-breasted, with two rows of eight buttons, the distance between the rows narrowing from 2½in. at the top to 1½in. at the bottom. Collars, pointed cuffs and turnbacks were of the colour of the regimental facings. At the rear centre of the skirts the jackets had vertical pleats, flanked by three buttons on each side, and surmounted by the so-called 'waterfalls' in lace colour.

The 3rd, 4th and 14th Light Dragoons had scarlet facings; the 13th had pale buff, acknowledged in 1843 as being nearly white. Officers' jackets had gilt buttons, bullion back-pieces, gold epaulettes, and ⅝in. wide gold braid edging the collars and cuffs, embellished according to rank with gold Russia braid tracing. Other Ranks' jackets were similar in both style and colour; they had pewter regimental buttons, and yellow braid on the collars and cuffs (the 13th Light Dragoons had no yellow braid from 1843). Their brass shoulder scales were retained by narrow brass bridles.

Officers' girdles were faced with gold lace, with two crimson silk stripes, and gold loops and olives; Other Ranks had similar girdles of yellow webbing with two red stripes, and yellow cord loops and olives; all girdles had leather fastening straps and buckles beneath the loops and olives. Officers' Dress trousers were dark blue with two gold lace bands up the outward seams; their Undress trousers,

---

THE PLATE

FIGURES:

Top left: *Field Officer in Dress, 13th Light Dragoons; Officer, 14th Light Dragoons, Indian Service dress.*
Centre, left to right: *Sergeant Major, 13th Light Dragoons, Undress, Crimea; Trumpeter, 13th Light Dragoons; Adjutant, 4th Light Dragoons, in Undress.*
Top right: *Corporal, 13th Light Dragoons, Crimea field dress; Private, 4th Light Dragoons, in Dress.*
Bottom left: *Sergeant Major, 3rd Light Dragoons, in stable dress.*
Bottom right: *Sergeant, 14th Light Dragoons, Indian service dress.*

DETAILS:

Top centre: *Officers' shako, 13th Light Dragoons; Other Ranks' shako, 14th Light Dragoons; Officers' Dress sabretache, above Officers' shako plate, 14th Light Dragoons; Officers Undress and Dress pouch belts and pouches.*
Centre left: *White calico shako cover for hot climates; Officers' black oilskin foul weather cover; hilt, 1822 pattern Light Cavalry Officers' sabre; epaulette with Lieutenant-Colonel's badge of rank; Officers' peaked forage cap; Sergeant Majors' forage cap.*
Centre right: *Other Ranks' pouch belt and pouch; girdle; hilt, 1829 pattern Light Cavalry sabre; scale epaulette; forage cap; red bandsman's forage cap, 4th Light Dragoons.*
Bottom centre: *Officers' jacket, 3rd Light Dragoons, with collar, cuff and rear skirt details; Officers' girdle; rear detail, trumpeters' jacket, 3rd Light Dragoons; Other Ranks' jacket, Corporal, 4th Light Dragoons, with cuff and rear skirt detail.*

Plate XX 7

and the trousers of Other Ranks, had two yellow stripes. Officers and Other Ranks of the 13th Light Dragoons wore grey trousers in the Crimea; their Officers' Undress trousers, and Other Ranks' trousers, had two white stripes. During the Crimean campaign black leather strapping and booting was added to all trousers.

All ranks had blue cloaks with scarlet linings and facing colour collars. Trumpeters' jackets and stable jackets were distinguished by facing colour pipings in the back and sleeve seams; they wore fancy forage caps, and had red shako plumes. Yellow trumpet badges sewn on facing colour cloth were worn on the right upper sleeves. Although armed with revolvers, they appear not to have worn the pouch belt.

The Officers' Dress sword belt was faced with 1¼in. wide gold lace, with edging and a ¼in. wide central stripe of facing colour silk. The belt was fastened with a gilt snake clasp, and had two sword slings and three slings for the sabretache. The Dress sabretache had a deep red Morocco leather pocket some 12½in. deep by 10½in. wide at the bottom and 8in. wide at the top; the larger face was of blue cloth edged with 2¼in. wide gold lace. In the centre were laurel sprays with scrolls bearing battle honours enclosing the Royal Cypher. The Officers' pouch belt was faced with 2in. wide gold lace with a ½in. wide central stripe of facing-colour silk; it had engraved silver plates with chains and pickers, buckle, tip and slide, and was attached to the pouch by silver buckles and rings. The pouch box was of black leather with a gold-embroidered edge. The solid silver flap, 7½in. wide by 2¼in. deep, had an engraved edge, and the Crown and Royal Cypher in raised gilt. In Undress, Officers wore a black patent leather sword belt with black slings and a gilt snake clasp; the Undress sabretache was also of plain black patent leather.

Officers were armed with the 1822 pattern Light Cavalry sabre, with a steel half-basket hilt, black fishskin grip bound with silver wire, and a steel scabbard. The sword knot was gold and crimson cord with an acorn end. Other Ranks were generally armed with the 1821/1829 pattern sword; this had a three-bar steel guard, and the steel ears of the solid backstrap were clipped to the sides of the black grip. In 1853 a new pattern of sword for Other Ranks was approved; this also had a three-bar guard, but the black leather grip was rivetted through the tang. Both the 1829 and 1853 pattern swords had steel scabbards and white leather sword knots. The later pattern is unlikely to have been issued to the cavalry in the Crimea. Officers and senior NCOs were armed with revolvers of various patterns. Other Ranks were armed with the Lovell 'Victoria' pattern percussion carbine, carried attached by a swivel hook to the pouch belt.

XXI

1854

2nd (Royal North British) Regiment of Dragoons

By 1854 the tall bearskin caps of the 1830s and 1840s had been reduced to a height comparable to those of the Foot Guards. The plume had been similarly reduced. and was now 9in. long, secured in a grenade-shaped socket on the left side. The caps had chin chains mounted on leather straps: and a metal badge in the shape of the White Horse of Hanover sunk into the fur low on the rear. Trumpeters' caps had longer. deep red feather plumes.

The Undress caps were dark blue. and had the regiment's distinctive 'vandyke' or zig-zag lace band. in gold for Officers and senior NCOs. in white for junior ranks. The Officers' caps had angled black leather peaks edged with gold embroidery. and a gold button centred in a figure of tracing on the top.

The coatees were single-breasted. scarlet for Officers. senior NCOs and Sergeants. and red for Corporals and Privates. The ends of the collars were decorated with two broad lace loops: and the cuffs with a single doubled chevron of lace with a central button. Since 1846 the skirts had been shortened so that they just reached the saddle when the soldier was mounted. Officers had rich gold lace. senior NCOs and Sergeants cheaper gold lace. and junior ranks yellow lace. Officers' coatees had nine front buttons. Other Ranks' coatees eight: regimental buttons were gilt for Officers and pewter for Other Ranks.

Other distinctive features of Officers' coatees were the large flaming grenade ornaments worn centred. horizontally. on the collar loops. and smaller but similar grenade ornaments worn on the junctions of their turnbacks. Mansion. Eschauzier and M. A. Hayes all show gold grenades mounted on blue cloth. The collar grenades were not worn by NCOs or Privates: but General Pajol's sketches (Brunon Collection) confirm that they wore yellow. lozenge-shaped turnback ornaments. mounted on blue cloth. with either buttons or small grenades in the centres.

The Officers' gold bullion epaulettes were of the pattern common to all Dragoon Regiments. and had gold embroidered straps and crescents mounted on blue facing cloth. and bearing silver embroidered regimental grenade badges on the pads. A lacemaker's old pattern book gives gold straps. gilt crescents and silver grenades. and this is confirmed by examination of photographs in the National Army Museum Collection. A painting by Dubois Drahonet. albeit of 1832. also appears to show a silver grenade. At this period rank badges were still worn only by Field Officers: a silver Crown and Star. a Crown. and a Star for Colonel. Lieutenant Colonel and Major respectively. Captains and Subaltern Officers wore no badges and were virtually indistinguishable.

Other Ranks wore solid brass shoulder scales without badges. the solid crescent ends projecting

---

THE PLATE

FIGURES:

Top left: *Field Officer in Dress uniform; Private.*
Centre: *Captain in Drill Order; Sergeant at Varna, 1854 (after Pajol).*
Top right: *Corporal in Marching Order; Major, Crimean campaign dress.*
Bottom left: *Regimental Sergeant Major in stable jacket.*
Bottom right: *Private in stable jacket.*

DETAILS:

Top centre: *Officers' sash, Dress sabretache, Dress pouch belt and pouch, waist belt plate and button; Trumpeters' sword.*
Centre left: *Officers' Undress sabretache, pouch belt and pouch, sword belt and slings, coatee collar and cuff detail; hilt of Officers' sword.*
Centre right: *Other Ranks' equipment; 1821-1830 (left) and 1853 pattern sword hilts; and Medusa-head NCOs' sword knot button shown by Pajol.*
Bottom centre: *Officers' coatee, with turnback detail; forage caps of Officer, senior NCOs and Other Ranks; Trumpeters' bearskin, bearskin plume socket ornament, bearskin back badge, Other Ranks' button; Field Officers' epaulette, Other Ranks' shoulder scales, Troop Officers' epaulette; Other Ranks' coatee with turnback detail.*

Plate XXI 6

beyond the shoulder seam; the heavy scales were secured by lacing through four holes in the coat shoulder. Trumpeters were distinguished by special shoulder scales with stamped brass grenades and short, simulated fringing in brass.

In May 1850 Horse Guards had issued a Circular Memorandum (No.22) which set out in official terms the badges of rank to be worn by NCOs of Heavy Cavalry: Regimental Sergeant Major, a Crown over a four-bar double lace chevron; Troop Sergeant Major, a Crown over a three-bar double lace chevron; Sergeant, a three-bar double lace chevron; Corporal, a two-bar double lace chevron. The Crown was worked in gold and coloured silks, and the chevrons were gold lace. The RSM's chevrons are likely to have been slightly broader than those of the Troop Sergeant Majors. Lance Corporals had a single chevron of double-bar lace. All NCOs' badges of rank were worn on the upper right sleeve only.

Officers' Dress trousers had 1¼in. wide gold lace laid over the outward seams; from 1850, their Undress trousers had yellow cloth stripes matching those worn by Other Ranks. Officers' Dress spurs were brass, but for Undress they wore steel, matching those of Other Ranks.

In the Crimea, plumes, epaulettes and shoulder scales were all laid aside; and it is said that gauntlet gloves were also not worn. Black leather strapping and booting for the trousers were provided for all ranks, although Pajol does not show this addition in his sketches.

By 1854 the Officers' Dress pouch belts were laced with the full scalloped 'Thistle' pattern as used on the sabretache, and not the 'S and Rose' pattern which had previously been in use. In the Crimea the Officers wore the Undress white leather belts. NCOs and junior ranks wore the pouch belt and sword belt with slings; Sergeants, Corporals and Privates wore carbine spring swivels on their pouch belts, but Sergeant Majors and Trumpeters did not.

Officers were armed with the 1834 pattern sword with the 'honeysuckle' pattern pierced steel guard lined with buckskin, carried in a steel scabbard. Some NCOs and men were issued with the newly-introduced 1853 pattern sword with a steel three-bar guard, rivetted grip and steel scabbard; but most were armed with the 1821-1830 pattern weapon with a large steel solid bowl guard, bound grip and steel scabbard. Musicians and Trumpeters probably retained their old Mameluke pattern swords with lions'-head pommels.

Sergeants and junior ranks were also armed with the Lovell 'Victoria' side lock percussion carbine with swivel rammer; Sergeant Majors and Trumpeters carried revolvers. Officers were also armed with revolvers of various patterns including Colt, Adams and Tranter.

(Thanks are extended to Messrs. R. J. Harris and W. Y. Carman for providing invaluable information for the preparation of this plate.)

XXII

1854

Royal Regiment of Artillery

The Royal Regiment of Artillery was formed in 12 Battalions each of eight companies. In time of war companies were designated as Field or Instruction Batteries. or were retained as Garrison units. There were. in addition. seven troops of Horse Artillery. Eight Field Batteries and a Siege Train embarked for the Crimea. with two troops of Horse Artillery.

The 1843 pattern shako was made of felt. 7in. high and 8in. in diameter. with a 1in. leather upper rim. The front peak was 2½in. deep. the rear 1¼in. deep: there was an inch-broad band around the base. with a buckle at the rear. The cap had a brass chin chain mounted on leather: and an upright white horsehair plume rose out of a grenade-shaped socket with the Crown and Cypher on the ball. The Officers' cap plate differed from that of the Other Ranks in having 'UBIQUE' on a scroll below the Gun. full mantling to the Arms. and a curved scroll at the base. The Other Ranks plate had 'UBIQUE' above the Gun.

Officers' forage caps were dark blue with black peaks. gold lace bands and gold top buttons. Junior ranks had peakless caps. with red bands and red pipings round the crown: Sergeants and Staff Sergeants had 1¼in. gold lace bands: NCOs were to have small chevrons of rank fixed above the cap bands in front. but some photographs show none.

Officers' dark blue coatees had 2½in. deep scarlet collars and cuffs. Collar and cuff flap embroidery was of a gold foliage pattern: gold flaming grenade ornaments were stitched to the collar embroidery. and at the junctions of the scarlet turnbacks. The coatee had two rows of ten gilt buttons on the front and two buttons at the rear of the waist. Other Ranks wore coatees of similar style and colours. The collars and cuff flaps were trimmed with ½in. wide yellow worsted lace. and there were yellow grenades on the collars. Staff Sergeants and Sergeants had gold lace and grenades. Buttons were brass: and one was set at the junction of each pair of turnbacks.

Officers wore two bullion epaulettes with the special badge of three Guns in a Garter inscribed 'UBIQUE' with the Crown overall. Field Officers wore silver badges of rank on the straps in the usual sequence. It is not clear whether Field Officers wore the above-mentioned Gun and Garter badge with the usual oval bearing the Royal Cypher. used by Field Officers of other corps. since it appears impossible to include all these badges on the strap simultaneously. Colonels and Lieutenant Colonels had bullions 3½in. in length. Majors 3in.. and other Officers 2½in. Junior ranks had red straps edged with yellow lace. yellow bridles. and yellow crescents and fringes. Staff Sergeants and Sergeants had gold lace round the straps. gold bridles. gold crescents and yellow fringes – probably gold for the former.

Bombardiers and Corporals had one and two yellow worsted chevrons. Sergeants three gold chevrons. all worn on both upper sleeves. It is not clear precisely what badges Staff Sergeants and Battery Sergeant Majors wore at this period. but a photograph by Roger Fenton shows a senior NCO

THE PLATE

FIGURES:

Top left: *Company Sergeant at Varna, Bulgaria, 1854.*
Top right: *Bombardier, with linstock.*
Centre, left to right: *Field Officer in Levee Dress; Staff Sergeant (after Fenton); Battery Officer in Undress.*
Bottom left: *Battery Sergeant, Marching order (valise on the limber).*
Bottom right: *Gunner in shell jacket and forage cap.*

DETAILS:

Top centre: *Officers' shako, Other ranks' shako, flanking Other Ranks' shako plate, set over Field Officers' (left) and Battery Officers' swords, and Officers' sash, above Officers' waist belt plate.*
Centre left: *Knapsack, with blanket, mess tin and greatcoat; epaulettes (left to right) of Sergeant, Captain, and Gunner.*
Centre right: *Officers' forage cap; Victoria carbine; 1853 Artillery carbine; Sergeants' and Other Ranks' forage caps.*
Bottom centre: *Gunners' coatee, with button, and rear detail; Officers' shell jacket, with shoulder cord detail; Officers' coatee, with collar, cuff flap, and rear detail, and button.*

Plate XXII 30

with gold chevrons just above his right cuff. Company Sergeants – the equivalents of Colour Sergeants of Infantry – wore the Colour Badges on both sleeves.

Officially abandoned in 1854, but still worn in the Crimea, the Officers' frock coat was in the process of replacement by the shell jacket. Sergeants and men had shell jackets with scarlet collars and blue cuffs, with a single row of 14 buttons on the front and one on each cuff; yellow or gold twisted cords were worn on the shoulders.

Trousers were dark blue with 2in. red stripes; Officers' sashes were crimson silk, knotted on the left (or on the right, when mounted). Senior NCOs had crimson worsted sashes knotted on the left. Other Ranks had dark blue greatcoats with capes; Sergeants had red collars and cuffs. Officers had blue capes lined scarlet, with gilt clasps at the neck.

In Review Order the shako was worn with the coatee and blue trousers with red stripes. The sash was worn knotted on the left, with the sword belt over it. NCOs and men also wore the shako, coatee, blue trousers with red stripes, waist belt, and pouch belt. In Field Day order the dress was the same, but the Other Ranks wore the greatcoat folded on their backs. In Heavy Marching Order the shakos of all ranks were ordered to be worn in oilskin covers; Other Ranks carried the knapsack, with the greatcoat folded square on the outside of the flap, with the mess tin buckled on top.

On the march and in the field, Officers wore the forage cap and frock coat, the sash and black waist belt. NCOs and men of the marching element had the greatcoat rolled and buckled on top of the knapsack and the mess tin buckled on the flap. Light Marching Order was almost the same, but the greatcoat was folded and placed in the knapsack, together with a change of shirt, a spare pair of stockings, the shaving kit and the shoe brushes. On the march and in the field the men of the Field Batteries strapped their knapsacks and mess tins on to the limbers, together with blankets, corn sacks, and their greatcoats, folded one over the other with the greatcoats on top. On their person they carried the haversack and canteen. Mounted NCOs, Gunners and Artificers carried saddle bags on the pads behind them, with their mess tins buckled on top. The blankets were folded under the saddles, and the greatcoats were folded and buckled over the holsters.

Officers were armed with 1822 pattern Infantry swords with gilt hilts. Field Officers had brass scabbards, Battery Officers steel scabbards, and all Officers gilt-mounted black scabbards for Court attendance and similar occasions. Knots were crimson and gold. Swords were carried on waist belts with gilt plates. Gunners were armed with the 1853 rifled Artillery carbine and sword bayonet; Sergeants of Field Batteries were armed with the Victoria carbine carried on Light Cavalry style pouch belts with swivels.

(Our thanks to W. Y. Carman for his assistance in preparing this plate.)

XXIII

1856

Infantry of the Line: Officers

In January 1855 a new Infantry headdress was introduced. replacing the 'Albert' shako which had been in use since 1843-44. The new cap was smaller and lighter. and. with its slightly forward-tilted top. resembled the French infantry cap of the period. Known as the 'second Albert' shako. the Officers' pattern was 5½in. high at the front. 7½in. high at the back. and tapered inwards towards the top. The leather top surface was sunken. but the leather was brought up and turned over the upper edge and stitched to make a ⅜in. black leather top band. The front peak was about 2⅜in. deep. bound and stitched around the edge and slightly angled downwards. There was a 1⅜in. wide rear peak which was much more sharply angled. continuing the line of the back of the shako. which was made to come around the sides of the cap to join the front peak. below a black leather band. A black patent leather chin strap with a buckle on the right side was secured to the inside edges of the cap.

The 2in. diameter woollen ball tufts were two-thirds white over one-third red for Regimental Field Officers and Officers of Battalion Companies: all green for Light Infantry companies: and all white for Grenadier Companies. (Battalion Company Officers of the 34th Regiment of Foot had ball tufts half red over half white: the Light Infantry Company of the 46th Regiment had all red tufts.) The tufts were mounted in gilded. leafed sockets. A bronze Gorgon's head fitting at the upper rear of the cap served as a ventilator. The shako plate was a gilded eight-point star surmounted by the Crown. which covered the upper point: the plate measured approximately 3⅜in. across the widest dimension. and about 4⅛in. high including the Crown. In the centre was the Garter. bearing the Motto. enclosing the pierced regimental number. stencil cut. on a black velvet backing. In some regiments the ancient badge or device was added to the numerals. and in others the badge or device was used in place of the numerals.

The Austrian system of identifying rank on the shako was now introduced. Colonels and Lieutenant Colonels had two bands of ½in. wide gold lace around the upper part of the shako. and Majors a single band of the same lace. In Fusilier and Light Infantry Regiments grenade and bugle-horn badges continued to be worn: and in 1857 a drooping white or green horsehair plume was introduced to replace their tufts. although the 5th Fusiliers were permitted their red over white distinction.

The Officers' 1855 pattern dark blue Undress forage cap had a black oak leaf pattern braid band. except in Royal Regiments. which wore a scarlet cloth band. and Scottish Regiments. which wore a diced band. It had a black cord button and a braid figure on top. and a narrow black leather chin strap. On the band was displayed the regimental number. usually in Arabic numerals but in some cases in Roman figures. Ancient badges or devices were alternatively worn. principally by the 1st. 2nd. 3rd. 4th. 6th. 8th. 9th. 18th and 27th Regiments.

THE PLATE

Left. top to bottom:
Tunic. Colonel, 11th (North Devonshire) Regiment.
Tunic, Lieutenant Colonel, 97th (Earl of Ulster's) Regiment. with rear skirt detail.
Tunic, Major, 48th (Northamptonshire) Regiment.
Centre. top to bottom:
1822 pattern sword in gilt-mounted black leather scabbard – note Undress knot; shakos of a Major, a Colonel, and a Company Officer, set over 1822 pattern swords in brass and steel scabbards, with Dress knots, and Officers' sash; shako plate of 48th Regiment; Officers' sword belt.

Colonel, 56th (West Essex) Regiment.
Major, 76th Regiment, in Undress.

Undress caps of 2nd (Queen's Royal) and (right) 3rd (East Kent) Regiments, flanking shell jacket of Captain, 34th (Cumberland) Regiment, with rear waist and button detail; silver-embroidered Crown and Bath Star rank badges; button of 9th (East Norfolk) Regiment, with regimental lace loop.
Right. top to bottom:
Tunic, Captain, 58th (Rutlandshire) Regiment.
Tunic, Lieutenant, 18th (Royal Irish) Regiment, with rear skirt detail.
Tunic, Ensign, 17th (Leicestershire) Regiment.

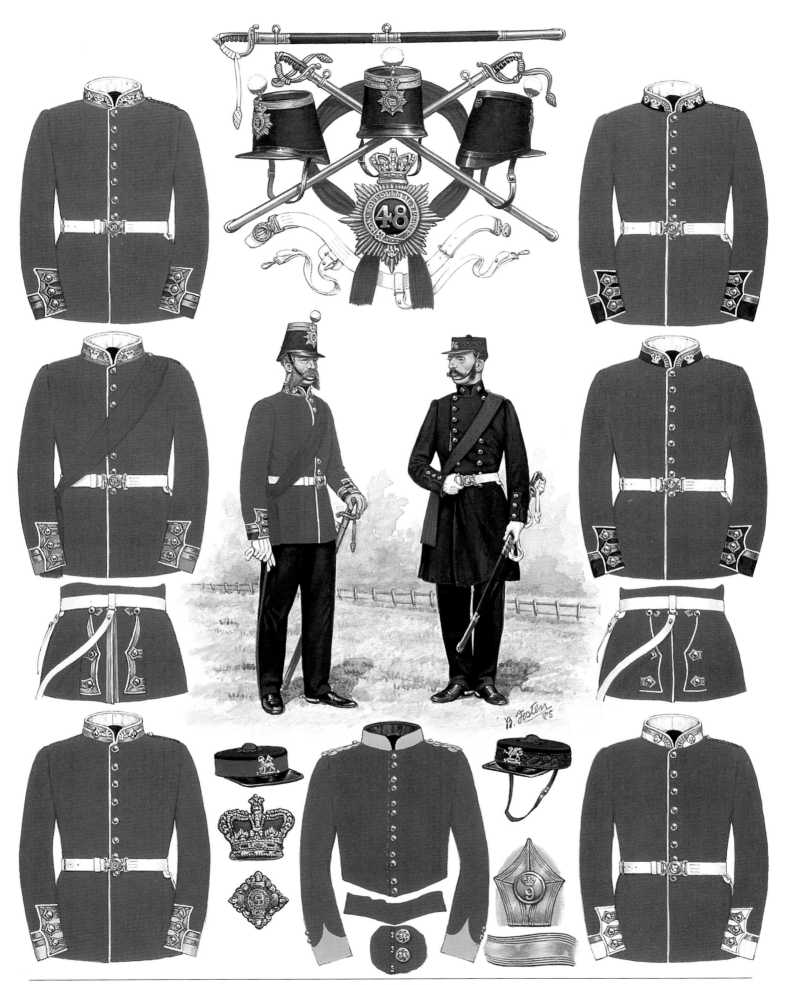

Plate XXIII 8

The 1856 pattern single-breasted tunic replaced the ugly 1855 double-breasted coat. Collars, cuffs and cuff flaps were in the regimental facing colour; and the buttons were gilded, of regimental pattern. Badges of rank were silver-embroidered, and were now worn on the collars: a Crown and Star for Colonels and Captains; a Crown for Lieutenant Colonels and Lieutenants; and a Star for Majors and Ensigns. Field Officers were distinguished from Company Officers by ½in. wide gold lace all around the collars, on the cuff flaps and rear skirt slashes, and in two bands around the top of the cuffs. Captains and Subalterns had a single ½in. gold lace around the outer edges of the collars, and a single band around the cuffs. The tunics had a crimson silk cord on the left shoulder only, to retain the crimson silk sash now worn from the left shoulder to the right hip.

In Undress either a scarlet shell jacket or a dark blue frock coat was worn. The shell jacket had collar and pointed cuffs in regimental facing colour, and gold 'basket weave' cords on both shoulders. Although most regiments had adopted by this date shell jackets with ten buttons equally spaced down the front, others retained the old hooked pattern with buttons set in pairs or at equal intervals. The frock had a crimson silk twisted cord on the left shoulder only; it had two buttons set in the waist at the rear, and two more on the vertical pocket slashes.

Paymasters, Quartermasters and Surgeons wore the uniform of the regiment with cocked hats, black waist belts, but not the sash. The Paymaster had no feather, the Quartermaster a 3½in. feather, and the Surgeon a drooping black cock's tail. The Surgeon also had a black leather shoulder belt with a small case for instruments.

In summer indigo trousers with scarlet welts were worn, but in winter these were replaced by trousers of Oxford mixture, also with scarlet welts. The trousers tapered from thigh to ankle. Mounted Officers wore trousers strapped under the instep. Brass screwed spurs were worn by Field Officers for Dress, but steel for Undress; steel spurs were also worn by Adjutants.

Sword belts were of white enamelled leather, with a sword carriage and gilt hook. The plate was the Union locket with a round gilt clasp, having in its centre the regimental number surmounted by the Crown, or a badge, all in silver, with the title of the regiment on the circlet. The sword was the 1822 pattern with a gilt half-basket hilt and the Queen's Cypher inserted in the outward bars, lined with black patent leather; the grip was black fishskin bound with a spiral of three gilt wires. Regimental Field Officers had brass, Adjutants steel, and Company Officers black leather scabbards, the latter with gilt mounts; this was also carried by all Officers attending Court or similar ceremonial functions. The sword knots were gold and crimson, with gold acorns.

XXIV

1856

Infantry of the Line:
Non-Commissioned Officers and Privates

The Infantry shako approved on 16 January 1855, generally called the 'second Albert' pattern, was made of coarse felt for NCOs and junior ranks. It had a depth of 5½in. at the front and 7⅛in. at the back, the sunken leather top surface being lapped over the upper edge and stitched to form a ⅜in. top band. A ⅝in. wide band stitched along both sides reinforced the bottom edge. The 2⅜in. deep front peak and more sharply angled 1⅜in. deep rear peak met at the sides in a continuous line. A black leather chin strap, buckled on the right, was attached inside the bottom edges; there were black circular ventilators at the top of each side. A 2in. diameter woollen ball tuft was mounted in a socket at the centre of the top front edge. The tuft was white for Grenadier, green for Light Infantry, and two-thirds white over one-third red for Battalion companies. (In 1858 Flank Companies within Infantry Battalions were abolished, and the Grenadier and Light Infantry Company distinctions disappeared). The plate was brass, cast in one piece, as an eight-point star with the top point obscured by the Crown. The Garter, inscribed with the Motto, encircled brass pierced regimental numerals on a black backing.

In March 1856 the first, double-breasted tunic was replaced by a smarter single-breasted pattern with shorter skirts. Staff Sergeants and Sergeants had scarlet tunics, and junior ranks, red. The Sergeant Major, Quartermaster Sergeant, Instructor of Musketry, Drum Major and Band Sergeant all wore four chevrons as badges of rank. The Sergeant Major's chevrons were surmounted by a Crown; the Musketry Instructor's by crossed rifles; and the Drum Major's by a drum. The Schoolmaster and Bandmaster Sergeant wore no chevrons, but the latter had gold cord shoulder knots. Senior NCOs' chevrons were of doubled gold lace. Colour Sergents had one white chevron surmounted by the Union Flag, crossed swords and Crown on the right sleeve, and three white chevrons on the left sleeve. Sergeants had three chevrons of white worsted lace; if the Paymaster Sergeant or Orderly Room Sergeant ranked as Colour Sergeants, they wore gold lace chevrons. Corporals wore two chevrons of white worsted lace, and Lance Corporals one. All chevrons were sewn to a backing of regimental facing colour. Light Infantry, Fusiliers and Highlanders wore badges of rank on both upper sleeves; all other NCOs, on the right sleeve only. Buttons were brass, and of regimental patterns. Staff Sergeants and Sergeants wore crimson worsted sashes over the right shoulder. Good Conduct badges were of white worsted lace, and took the form of upwards-pointing chevrons of single width, not doubled like those used in badges of rank, sewn above the right cuff, without facing colour backing. The lace which trimmed the seams and wings of Drummers was of a special pattern for each regiment; it often

---

THE PLATE

Left, top to bottom:
Tunic, Sergeant Major, 45th (Nottinghamshire) Regiment.
Tunic, Colour Sergeant, Light Infantry Company, 46th (South Devonshire) Regiment.
Canteen, haversack and bayonet frog.
Tunic, Lance Corporal, 17th (Leicestershire) Regiment.
Centre, top to bottom:
1855 shako with Grenadier (left) and Light Infantry Company tufts, between Sergeant Majors' sword belt and sword, flanking Other Ranks' shako plate; Other Ranks' waistbelt locket and clasp, set over Sergeants' sash, above Other Ranks' waist belt, and expense pouch.

Private, 39th (Dorsetshire) Regiment, Review Order.
Sergeant Major, 2nd (Queen's Royal) Regiment, Review Order.

Colour Sergeants' badge, above Other Ranks' shell jacket of a Royal Regiment, between forage caps of (left) Sergeant Major or Staff Sergeant, 16th (Bedfordshire) Regiment and Other Ranks of 22nd (Cheshire) Regiment; respresentative shoulder straps; button detail.
Right, top to bottom:
Tunic, Sergeant, 41st (The Welsh) Regiment.
Tunic, Corporal, 22nd (Cheshire) Regiment.
Knapsack, with rolled blanket, mess tin in cover, cartridge pouch and belt, percussion cap pouch.
Tunic, Private, 95th (Derbyshire) Regiment, rear view.

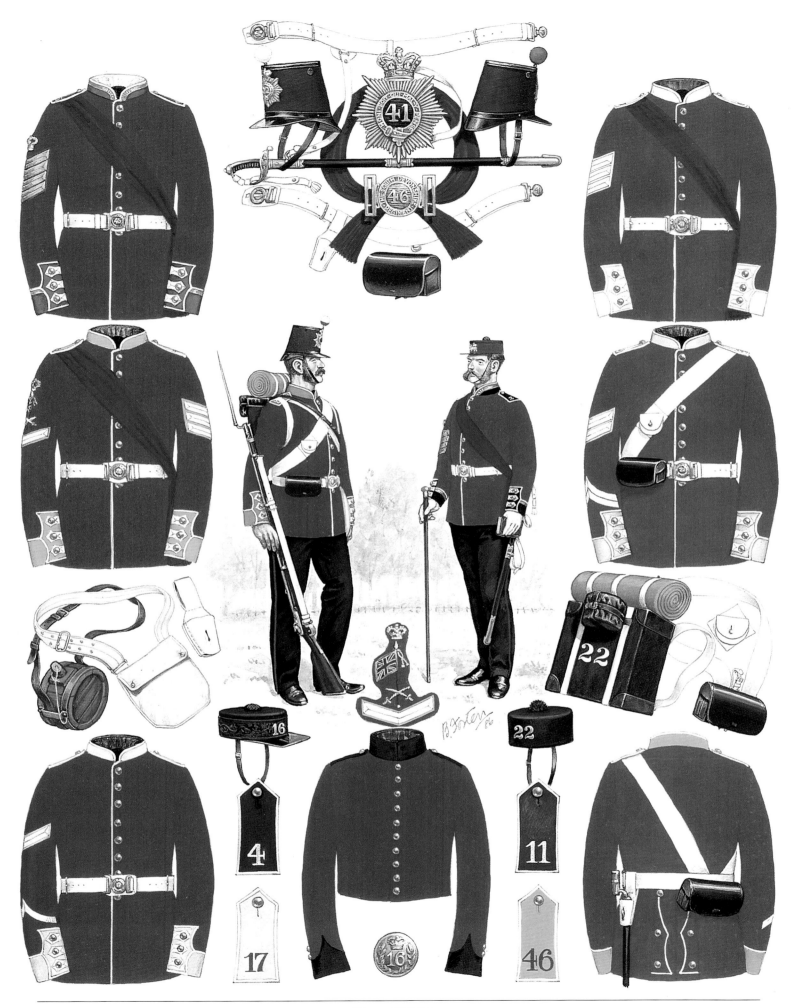

Plate XXIV 16

reflected either the regimental lace worn since the 18th century, or the livery lace of the person who had raised the regiment.

Oxford mixture heavyweight trousers, with scarlet welts up the outward seams, were worn in winter. In summer dark blue trousers with scarlet welts were worn, except on hot stations, where white linen trousers were substituted.

Infantry equipment was of the pattern approved in 1850. The 2in. wide adjustable waist belt was of whitened buffalo leather, with a brass locket and clasp fastening, the clasp approximately 1⅞in. in diameter and inscribed with the regimental title while the central locket bore the regimental number. Adjustment was by two brass buckles and leather keeps; and a brass D-ring near the centre of the back connected by a small buckled strap to the cartridge pouch, to steady it. The 17in. socket bayonet was carried in a V-shaped leather frog on the left side of the belt; Sergeants, however, had 22¾in. sword bayonets carried in movable frogs.

The 2¼in. wide whitened buffalo leather pouch belt was worn over the left shoulder, supporting a black leather cartridge pouch approximately 8in. in 4½in. by 3in. deep. Lined with metal, the pouch initially carried 60 rounds, and was fitted with an inner metal compartment for ten percussion caps. Sergeants were provided with smaller pouches holding 20 rounds. By 1855 the 60-round pouch was being replaced by a 40-round main pouch, and for manoeuvres and active service a black leather 'expense' pouch holding an additional 20 rounds was fitted to the right front of the belt; the small leather percussion cap pouch previously worn in that position now moved to the front of the pouch belt. (From 1859 the main pouch held 50 rounds, the expense pouch ten rounds, an oil bottle and cleaning materials.)

The knapsack was made of japanned canvas on a rigid wooden frame, with stout leather corner pieces; it measured approximately 13in. high by 15in. wide and 4in. deep. It was carried on white leather shoulder straps, connected until 1856 by a horizontal breast strap. The semi-circular metal mess tin, in a black canvas cover, attached to the knapsack straps by a black leather strap. On top of the knapsack three narrow white buckled straps enabled a rolled greatcoat or blanket to be attached. The regimental number was painted in white on the outer surface of the knapsack. An unbleached linen haversack had a two-button flap, and a wide sling of the same material adjusted by a two-prong buckle. The blue-painted wooden water canteen, bound with iron hoops, had a buckled leather strap.

Staff Sergeants were armed with swords similar to the Officers' 1822 pattern, with polished brass mounts and white leather sword knots. Sergeants were armed with a shortened, 33in. barrel pattern of the Enfield .577 calibre percussion rifle. Other Ranks carried the 39in. barrel version, 10oz. heavier at 8lb. 14½oz., and sighted to 1,200 yards.

XXV

1868-1871

Infantry of the Line: Officers

The shako approved on 1 June 1869 (by General Order No.65) had a cork carcass covered with blue cloth, or with green for Light Infantry units. It was 4in. deep in front, 6½in. at the back, with a distinctive forward tilt, and a slightly sunken top surface. Around the upper edge were two bands of ¼in. gold braid, ¼in. apart: there was a single braid around the bottom edge, and single braids up the sides and centre back, which, with the ball tuft, gave it a very French appearance. For Colonels and Lieutenant Colonels two bands of ½in. wide gold lace around the top edge replaced the braids. A chin chain mounted on black velvet was suspended from 'rose' bosses. At the top rear of the cap was a gilt lion's-head and ring to which the chin chain was looped up for some Orders of Dress. The flat peak was of varnished black leather with a stitched edge. At the centre front of the top surface a woollen ball tuft was mounted in a gilt claw set on a ball inscribed with the Royal Cypher. The tuft was white over red: from 1870 Royal Regiments had all-red tufts: until 1874 Light Infantry Regiments wore hanging green plumes, replaced from that year by green tufts. The gilt plate, 3in. high by 3¼in. wide, was a laurel wreath surmounted by the Crown, with the Garter and Motto surrounding the regimental numerals cut out of a solid centre: several regiments had additional gold or silver regimental badges or devices.

The forage cap was the 1855 pattern flat-peaked type, with a black silk oakleaf-pattern band, and a black top button set in a figure of tracing. Royal Regiments had scarlet cloth bands: several regiments displayed approved badges in addition to the regimental numerals, and Light Infantry Regiments had bugle-horn badges.

The tunic was the pattern approved in 1868, scarlet, with collar and cuffs in cloth of the regimental facing colour. (The 50th (Queen's Own) Regiment wore its dark blue facings in velvet, a concession granted when the black velvet facings were replaced by blue in the reign of William IV). The collar was ornamented with ⅝in. gold lace along the top and front edge. The cuffs were pointed, with ⅜in. gold lace along the top edge and a tracing of gold Russia braid ¼in. above and below the lace: the lower tracings had a crowsfoot and eye, and the upper an Austrian knot reaching up the sleeve. The tunic had eight gilt regimental buttons in front and two at the waist behind. The skirts were closed, and two pleats descended from the rear waist buttons to the edge of the skirts. The front closure, the upper edge of the collar and the skirt pleats were edged with ¼in. wide white cloth. There was a hook-and-eye inside the lower front edge of the collar. On each shoulder was a doubled round gold cord, lined scarlet, and secured with a small button.

Field Officers had a row of braided eyes below the collar lace: and double lace around the top of the cuffs, showing a ¼in. 'light' of facing colour between. For Colonels and Lieutenant Colonels the Russia braiding above and below the cuff lace formed eyes: for Majors only the upper braid formed

---

THE PLATE

Left, top to bottom:
Tunic, Colonel, 2nd Battalion, 11th (North Devonshire) Regiment.
Tunic, Lieutenant Colonel, 58th (Rutlandshire) Regiment.
Tunic, Major, 47th (Lancashire) Regiment.
Shako, 68th (Durham Light Infantry) Regiment, c.1875.
Forage cap, 62nd (Wiltshire) Regiment.
Centre, top to bottom:
Shakos: (left) Field Officer, 8th (The King's) Regiment, c.1870; and (right) Company Officer of the Line; white leather (left) and gold-laced sword belts, with 1822 pattern swords; shako plate of 10th (North Lincolnshire) Regiment, above sword belt clasp of 70th (Surrey) Regiment, set on Officers' sash.

Captain, 1st Battalion, 6th (Royal 1st Warwickshire) Regiment, Levee Dress.
Lieutenant Colonel, 97th (Earl of Ulster's) Regiment, Review Order, c.1873.

White patrol jacket, Major, 38th (1st Staffordshire) Regiment.
1872 pattern scarlet frock, 22nd (Cheshire) Regiment.
Right, top to bottom:
Tunic, Captain, 76th Regiment.
Tunic, Lieutenant, 2nd Battalion, 18th (Royal Irish) Regiment – rear view for all ranks.
Tunic, Ensign, 16th (Bedfordshire) Regiment.
Forage cap, 18th (Royal Irish) Regiment.
Forage cap, 52nd (Oxfordshire Light Infantry) Regiment.

Plate XXV 22

eyes. For Captains the cuffs bore the double gold lace, but all collar and cuff braiding was plain, without eyes. Lieutenants and Ensigns had single gold lace between plain braiding on the cuffs. Embroidered silver rank badges were worn on the collars: for Colonels and Captains, a Crown and Star; for Lieutenant Colonels and Lieutenants, a Crown; for Majors and Ensigns, a Star. The crimson silk sash was worn over the left shoulder, knotted on the right hip above the sword belt. A wider gold sash with crimson stripes was worn with Levee Dress and on State occasions.

Paymasters, Quartermasters, Surgeons and Assistant Surgeons wore uniforms of their respective regiments with appropriate badges of rank, cocked hats, black patent leather waist belts, but no sashes. Paymasters had no feather in their hats; Quartermasters, a 3in. white feather with a red base (all green in Light Infantry Regiments); and Surgeons and Assistant Surgeons, black drooping cocks' tails. Surgeons and Assistants also wore a black patent leather shoulder belt with a small black instrument case ornamented with gilt appointments.

Ensigns became Sub-Lieutenants in 1871, and 2nd Lieutenants in 1877. From 1874 gold or silver regimental collar badges began to be taken into use by certain regiments, and were worn on the collar together with the rank badges.

Oxford mixture trousers with scarlet welts were worn in winter, dark blue scarlet-welted trousers in summer; dark blue trousers with two wide gold lace stripes flanking a crimson silk stripe were worn for Levee Dress and State occasions. Until 1872 mounted Field Officers and Adjutants wore overalls, and half-boots and buckled spurs.

Officers serving on hot weather stations wore the scarlet 'frock'. The pattern worn between 1864 and 1872 had a five-button front, and was edged with fine gold braid all round, with knots at the back of the collar, the heads of the hip vents, and on the cuffs. On the left breast was a set-in pocket edged with braid, or with an oblong flap. General Order No.71 of 1872 approved the revised pattern as illustrated in the plate, with white pipings and a facing-colour collar. A white or khaki version of the 1867 pattern braided patrol jacket was worn in India.

The sword was the 1822 pattern, modified in 1845. The gilt half-basket guard had the Royal Cypher set in the outward bars. The black scabbard with gilt mounts had largely been replaced by a steel scabbard by 1866. Field Officers had brass scabbards, and carried black leather sabretaches. Sword knots were crimson and gold, or white leather with a gold acorn for Undress. The belts were of 1½in. wide enamelled white leather, with inch-wide slings; a red Morocco belt, faced with gold lace with a central crimson stripe, was used for Levee Dress and on State occasions.

XXVI

1868-1871

Infantry of the Line: Non-Commissioned Officers and Privates

The last shako to be worn by NCOs and men was approved in June 1869. It was worn until 1878 by Service Companies, and by some Depot Companies until 1881. The shako was covered with dark blue cloth; around the upper and lower edges were stitched rows of red and black braid, and some regiments may have had additional braiding up the sides of the cap. The shako was approximately 4in. high in front, 6½in. at the back, and measured 6in. from front to back and 5½in. from side to side across the slightly sunken crown. The leather peak was flat; the brass chin chain, mounted on leather, was suspended from 'rose' bosses; and there was a small hook centrally placed at the top rear to which the chain could be looped. There were black ventilators in each side near the top edge. The woollen ball tuft, set in a brass fitting, was two-thirds white over one-third red; Royal Regiments had all red tufts from 1870. The shako plate, closely resembling that of the Officers' shako, was of stamped brass with the central regimental numerals voided. Until 1868 the Undress cap was the blocked Kilmarnock; thereafter the dark blue Glengarry was taken into use increasingly.

In the summer of 1868 a new tunic was introduced to replace the 1856 pattern, and the cuff flaps and pocket slashes of the previous pattern disappeared. The 1868 tunic was still scarlet for senior NCOs and Sergeants and red for Corporals and Privates; scarlet tunics for all ranks were approved in 1872. The round-fronted collar, tapered shoulder straps and pointed cuffs were in the regimental facing colour. The bottom edge of the collar, the left front, and the right front from the waist to the bottom edge, were piped white. The shoulder straps and the cuffs were edged with white braid, and the cuffs had a handsome white lace inner edging which showed a 'light' of facing colour between its upper edge and the edging braid. There were seven brass front buttons of regimental pattern, and two in the back of the waist on the vertical seams; two white pipings descended from these buttons to the bottom edge of the skirt.

Sergeant Majors had broad gold lace on the top and front edge of the collar, and replacing the white lace on the cuffs. In some regiments, Staff Sergeants had a narrower gold lace in the same positions. In 1866 the special Drummers' lace, differing in pattern from regiment to regiment, was replaced with a universal pattern of white with red crowns. The Drummers' tunics had red wings edged and barred with this lace, which was also laid over the coat seams, and in chevron form on the sleeves. Long Service and Good Conduct chevrons were worn on the right forearm by Other Ranks.

First battalions of the senior 25 regiments had white shoulder strap numerals surmounted by

---

THE PLATE

Top, left to right:
Tunic, Sergeant Major, 1st Battalion, 6th (Royal 1st Warwickshire) Regiment, 1868.
1869 shakos, front and rear, with (right) tuft of Royal Regiments; shako plate, above waist belt locket, 58th (Rutlandshire) Regiment, set over 1871 waist belt, Sergeants' sash; examples of distinctive regimental badges worn on Glengarry by (left) 22nd (Cheshire), and 58th (Rutlandshire) Regiments.
Tunic, Sergeant Instructor of Musketry, 2nd Battalion, 16th (Bedfordshire) Regiment, c.1871, with badge for Best Shot in Battalion.

Centre, left to right:
Tunic, Colour Sergeant, 1st Battalion, 22nd (Cheshire) Regiment, 1868, with badges for Best Shot in Battalion, and Sergeant of Best-Shooting Company. (Below) Lock detail, Snider-Enfield rifle.

Sergeant, 50th (Queen's Own) Regiment, Review Order c.1868.
Private, 76th Regiment, Drill Order c.1871.

Tunic, Private, 2nd Battalion, 17th (Leicestershire) Regiment, with pouch belt, percussion cap pouch and expense pouch of the Knapsack Equipment. (Below) Rear detail, all Other Ranks' tunics.

Bottom, left to right:
Tunic, front and rear, Lance Corporal, 39th (Dorsetshire) Regiment, c.1871, showing pouch of 1871 Valise Equipment as worn for Drill Order.
Kilmarnock forage cap; peaked Sergeant Majors' forage cap; Glengarry forage cap; regimental button, 22nd (Cheshire) Regiment, above universal pattern introduced 1871.
Frock front and rear, Private, 28th (North Gloucestershire) Regiment, c.1868, showing pleated fronts of early version.

Plate XXVI 13

'1B'; second battalions had red numerals below '2B'. Other regiments had white numerals without battalion distinction, but red numerals were used by white- and buff-faced regiments. In 1871 the distinctive cuff lace was abolished, and thereafter the white braid cuff edging was looped into trefoil knots up the sleeves. In March 1868 Sergeants and above were ordered to wear gold lace chevron badges; these were in the form of single bars of ½in. wide lace mounted directly on tunic cloth, edge to edge, without facing colour trimming. A General Order – No.55 of 1869 – directed Sergeant Majors and Quartermaster Sergeants to wear their badges of rank below the elbow. During this period some were worn points down, some points up. In about 1870, some regiments began using brass Crown collar badges.

As early as 1867 it had been mooted that Bandsmens' tunics should be red, but they continued to be white, with facing-colour distinctions, for several years.

By 1869 serge frocks began to be widely used for most duties. Early patterns had five-button fronts, rounded skirts, and in some cases deep pleats down each front. The backs were plain, with or without shallow hip vents. Some regiments had facing colour collars, or collars and shoulder straps, while others were quite plain. Shoulder straps and cuffs were edged with white braid, the latter looped into a single eye up the sleeves. NCOs' frocks became edged with a distinctive white braid.

Until 1871 the Infantry equipment comprised a 2in. wide whitened buff leather shoulder belt supporting a black leather cartridge pouch on the right hip, with a small leather percussion cap pouch stitched to the belt at the front; the ends of the belt tapered to fit buckles mounted on the rear of the pouch. The 2in. wide whitened buff leather adjustable waist belt had a brass union locket plate; a whitened buff leather 'ball bag' was worn on the right front, and a movable bayonet frog on the left hip; and a black expense pouch could be carried in the centre at the back. Sergeants wore smaller cartridge pouches than Other Ranks. The rigid-framed black canvas knapsack was carried high on the shoulders. Pioneers had white aprons, and were armed with saw-backed swords; they carried a variety of tools in specially designed cases, including axes, picks, shovels, billhooks and saws, and five of each battalion's Pioneers carried two gun-spikes.

In 1871 new equipment was approved, but issue was spasmodic. This was the 'First Valise Pattern'. A soft black canvas 'valise' (knapsack) was worn low on the back; white leather braces passed forward over the shoulder and down to chest level, where large brass rings were joined to three straps, two of which passed back round the body to the top and bottom of the valise, the third drooping to large D-rings on the waist belt. Two pouches were looped on to the waist belt at the front, and an expense pouch was suspended beneath the right pouch. Pouches were at first black, but buff patterns soon followed. When the valise was not worn its upper straps were buckled across the back.

The Sergeant Major, Quartermaster Sergeant and Staff Sergeant were armed with the 'Gothic' pattern sword as worn by Officers. Until 1871 Sergeants and Other Ranks were armed with the 1867 pattern Enfield rifle modified with the Snider breech; between 1871 and 1874 this weapon was replaced by the Martini-Henry, a true breech-loading rifle of .45in. calibre, which had a 22in. long socket bayonet to compensate for its shorter, 33in. barrel. Sergeants had sword bayonets with longer 'yataghan' blades.

XXVII

1879

24th (2nd Warwickshire) Regiment of Foot, Zulu War

The 24th Foot dated its origin to March 1689. when it was raised in Ireland. shortly to become Dering's Regiment. Its earliest active service consisted of various expeditions and actions under William of Orange. including the great siege of Namur in 1695. and service in the Brabant. During Marborough's campaigns it had three Colonels – initially John Churchill himself. followed by Brigadier Tatton and Colonel Primrose. The regiment fought with distinction at the Schellenberg. Blenheim. Ramillies. Oudenarde. Malplaquet. and in several smaller engagements. The 24th went on to establish a creditable record during the Seven Years' War. the American War of Independence. the French Revolutionary and Napoleonic Wars. the Sikh War and the Indian Mutiny. A second battalion was formed in 1858. and served in the Indian Ocean theatre and in India until 1873. It went out to South Africa in 1879. joining the senior battalion. which had been in the Cape Colony since 1875 and which had served in West Griqualand and in the Galeka War of 1877-78. Although nominally the 2nd Warwickshire Regiment. the 24th had had its Regimental Depot in Brecon since 1873. and Welsh influence was strong.

During the advance into Zululand of the Third or Centre Column of Lord Chelmsford's army. B Company. 2/24th. commanded by Lt. G. Bromhead. was left to defend the hospital and base camp at the mission station of Rorke's Drift close to the Buffalo River. For their part in the heroic defence of this post on 22/23 January 1879 Lt. Bromhead. Cpl. W. Allan. and Privates F. Hitch. H. Hook. 716 R. Jones and 1395 J. Williams rece.ved the Victoria Cross: Surgeon Major J. H. Reynolds of the Army Medical Department. attached to the 24th. was also awarded the Cross for his services during the action.

The 1/24th – less D and G Companies detached at Helpmakaar – and G Company with some other details of the 2/24th. were massacred at Isandlwana on 22 January. The detachment of the Centre Column at Isandlwana was commanded by Brevet Col. H. B. Pulleine. 1/24th: his staff included Lt. N. J. A. Coghill of his battalion. Capt. (Acting Maj.) W. Degacher was in command of the elements of the 1/24th present: the Adjutant. Lt. T. Melvill. the Paymaster. Maj. F. White. and Quartermaster J. Pullen were present with the headquarters. The companies were commanded as follows: A Coy.. Lt. F. P. Porteous: C Coy.. Lt. G. F. D. Hodson: E Coy.. Lt. C. W. Cavaye: F Coy.. Lt. J. P. Daly: and H Coy.. Lt. C. J. Atkinson. With G Coy.. 2/24th. and the other details of that battalion were Lt. C. D'A. Pope. the Adjutant Lt. H. J. Dyer. and Lt. F. Godwin-Austen. There were 402 non-commissioned officers and men of the 1/24th. plus the Band acting as stretcher-bearers. and 170 NCOs and men of the 2/24th. Attached to the 1/24th were six men of the 90th Regiment. three of the Army Service Corps. and Lt. Hall and ten men of the Army Hospital Department. There were only two 24th Regiment survivors. both bandsmen: Privates J. Bickley and E. Wilson. Lt. Melvill. being

---

THE PLATE

FIGURES:

Top left: *Sergeant Major: Company Officer wearing blue patrol.*
Centre: *Colour Sergeant and Company Officer. Marching Order.*
Top right: *Corporal and Private.*
Bottom left: *Sergeant.*
Bottom right: *Private. Marching Order.*

DETAILS:

Top centre: *Foreign Service Helmet. stained: 1868-78 pattern shako plate. still in use on helmets: Officers' and Other Ranks' waist belt lockets. flanking Glengarry badge. set over Officers' sash: Sergeants' (hilt left) and Other Ranks' bayonets.*
Centre left: *Other Ranks' Glengarry: Officers' forage cap. with both types of Sphinx badge: Officers' button: Other Ranks' collar and shoulder strap.*
Centre right: *Other Ranks' equipment as worn with valise: bayonet scabbard.*
Bottom centre. left to right: *Officers' India pattern frock (cuff design varied according to rank): Other Ranks' frock: Officers' blue patrol. with Lieutenant Colonel's rank badges.*

Plate XXVII 21

mounted at the time when the centre of the camp was being overrun by the Zulus, was ordered to save the Regimental Colour. He made for the river, being joined by Lt. Coghill. Coghill crossed in safety but, seeing Melvill unhorsed and in difficulties, turned back into the water to aid him, to be unhorsed in his turn. Both were overwhelmed and killed. The lost Colour, washed away by the river, was later recovered and was in use until 1933. Both Officers were subsequently awarded the Victoria Cross during the reign of King Edward VII when posthumous awards were instituted.

The headdress in Zululand in 1879 was the Foreign Service helmet, stained light brown; the helmet plates were ordered to be removed before entering Zululand, although some plates have been found at Isandlwana. On active service chin chains were replaced by leather chin straps. The Undress headdress for all ranks was the Glengarry, in dark blue with black ribbons and binding, dark blue tuft, and a distinctive regimental badge on the left front, gilded for Officers and in brass for Other Ranks. Alternatively Officers wore the peaked forage cap, bearing a gilt '24' surmounted by a Sphinx badge; this latter was of two types, one with the tail pointing up, the other with it pointing down.

Officers wore three types of coat: the India pattern scarlet frock, with regimental collar badges; the blue braided patrol; and a less frequently observed, simpler frock resembling the men's pattern, with neither pipings nor braid. Only Field Officers wore rank badges on the collar of the frock and the blue patrol. Other Ranks wore five-button scarlet frocks with green collar patches and green half-panel cuffs. The bottom edge of the collar, the shoulder straps, and the cuff panels were braided white, with white trefoil knots up the sleeves. The short skirts were rounded; the backs had two waist buttons, and two vertical white pipings to the bottom edge. (The waist buttons were often removed to prevent chafing by the equipment, and some frocks appear to have had plain backs with shallow hip vents. Shoulder numerals and collar badges were brass, and the brass buttons were of the universal pattern. Senior NCOs and Sergeants had gold chevrons; Lance Sergeants, Corporals and Lance Corporals, white chevrons. Officers and Sergeants normally wore crimson sashes over the left and right shoulders respectively, but none are shown in campaign photographs. Blue trousers with red welts were worn with black leather gaiters. Officers wore either canvas gaiters or various types of high boot.

Officers were armed with the modified 1822 pattern sword in a steel scabbard – brass, for Field Officers – carried on slings from leather sword belts with gilt lockets; the belt was worn under the blue patrol. Many Officers were additionally armed with revolvers in brown leather holsters. Other Ranks were armed with the Martini-Henry .45in. calibre breech-loading, single-shot rifle firing modified Boxer cartridges. The 1876 pattern triangular section socket bayonet had a black leather scabbard. Sergeants were armed with the 1871 pattern sword bayonet with steel hilt and chequered leather grips. The equipment was the 1871 Valise pattern, stained light brown, and worn in a variety of arrangements.

(Our thanks to Ian J. Knight of the Victorian Military Society for his generous help in the preparation of this plate.)

XXVIII

1881-c1894

Infantry of the Line: Officers

The blue cloth Home Service pattern spiked helmet was authorised for use by Officers and Other Ranks of the Infantry by General Order No.40 of May 1878. It had already been on trial by selected units for some time. There is little doubt that its design was based upon that of the *pickelhaube* worn in the German Army of the day. Officers' helmets had pointed front peaks bound with $\frac{3}{16}$in. wide gilded metal. The gilt spike was mounted on a handsome cruciform base; and there was a distinctive ¼in. wide convex metal bar down the centre of the back. From 1881 the gilded metal Crown and Star plate included a Wreath, a silver universal scroll inscribed with the territorial title, the Garter with its Motto, and a central circlet enclosing the Regimental Badge mounted on a coloured velvet or enamelled backing.

The straight-sided forage cap was introduced as Undress headdress in 1880 (General Order No.72) and replaced the cap with the large, flat, rectangular peak worn since 1855. The band was of black oakleaf-pattern braid, but of scarlet cloth for Royal Regiments and diced for Scottish Regiments. A dark blue Glengarry was authorised for Officers in 1868; the special badges for this headdress were backed with red cloth, and worn on the left side on a black silk cockade.

Prior to the sweeping 'Cardwell Reforms' of 1881 it had been decided to alter the position of Officers' badges of rank. Until 1880 they had been worn on the collars, but henceforth on the shoulder straps. In 1883 the system of badges was revised; the new scheme reserved the Crown for Field Officers. Colonels wore a Crown over two Stars; Lieutenant Colonels, a Crown and one Star; Majors, a Crown; Captains, two Stars; and Lieutenants, one Star. The rank of Second Lieutenant had no rank badges, the shoulder cords being quite plain. Officers of Militia wore a silver-embroidered 'M' below the rank badges.

English and Welsh Regiments had 'Rose', Scottish Regiments 'Thistle', and Irish Regiments 'Shamrock' pattern lace. The Norfolk, East Yorkshire, Leicestershire, East Surrey, York and Lancaster and Loyal North Lancashire Regiments, Somerset Light Infantry, and Connaught Rangers had distinctive black silk stripes in their lace. The tunic collars were now made higher, cut square in front, and hooked close. Field Officers' and Company Officers' tunics continued to differ in the disposition of lace and Russia braid on both collars and cuffs.

From 1881 English and Welsh Regiments had white facings, Scottish Regiments yellow, Irish Regiments green, and Royal Regiments blue. The Connaught Rangers, being the only non-Royal Irish Regiment, was thus the only regiment wearing green facings. In July 1885 the Berkshire Regiment became 'Royal' and consequently took blue facings. The Buffs (East Kent Regiment) and Suffolk Regiment had resumed their traditional facings by 1894.

Trousers were dark blue. Scarlet ¼in. wide welts were worn for everyday duty; but for State occasions, Balls, Royal Escort Duty or Guards of Honour Duty, 1½in. wide gold lace with a crimson

---

Plate XXVIII 1

silk central stripe was worn down the outward leg seams. Mounted Officers wore pantaloons, wide in the thigh and tight at the knee, with knee boots and jack spurs with straps, buckles and chains.

The crimson silk net sash was worn over the left shoulder, under the shoulder cord but over the waist belt, with the ends crossed through a runner at waist level and the fringe level with the bottom of the tunic. On State occasions, etc., when laced trousers or pantaloons were worn, a gold lace sash with two crimson silk stripes was substituted. Decorations and medals were worn over the sash on the left side of the tunic, in a horizontal line on a single bar.

A red Morocco leather belt faced with gold lace, with similar sword carriages and a gilt hook, was worn for State occasions, etc. On all other occasions the sword belt was of 1½in. wide white enamelled leather with similar sling and gilt hook. The plate and union locket for both types of belt had a circlet bearing the territorial title and the regimental badge on the central plate, and leafed bars. Field Officers had black leather sabretaches without metal ornaments for mounted duties. Sword belts were worn over the tunic but under the frock or the braided patrol jacket.

In October 1891 a new pattern of scarlet frock was approved for active service and manoeuvres. This had five front buttons, and rounded skirts; the high collar, shoulder straps and pointed cuffs were in facing colour. The plain back had vents on the hips; there were two breast, and two side patch pockets below the waist. Whistles were carried on scarlet lanyards. The dark blue braided patrol was provided with shoulder straps from 1881, and henceforth all Officers wore rank badges in gilt metal.

Greatcoats were medium grey, double-breasted, and reached to one foot above the ground. They had deep stand and fall collars, 6in. deep cuffs, two pockets at the waist, slash pockets to the rear, an opening at the rear with a fly and four buttons, two rows of six front buttons, and three buttons on each slashed flap. There was a cloth strap at the rear to confine the waist; the shoulder straps bore the badges of rank, and there was a slit on the left for the sword hilt. A detachable cape was worn.

The sword was the 1822 pattern with a gilt half-basket hilt with the Royal Cypher in the outward bars and lined with black patent leather. The grip was black fishskin bound with gilt wire; the scabbard was steel with two fixed rings. The Dress sword knot had a gold and crimson strap and a gold acorn; plain white leather knots were worn for Undress duties.

———◆•◆•◆———

XXIX

1881

Infantry of the Line:
Non-Commissioned Officers and Privates

The blue cloth spiked helmet approved in May 1878 had brass fittings for Other Ranks. Prior to 1881 the plate comprised the Crown and Star, the Garter with its Motto, a Wreath of laurel, and in the centre the regimental number on a cloth backing. Until supplies of these plates reached all regiments some continued to use the plates supplied with the last shako. In 1881 the numbered plates were replaced by a new pattern which had the territorial title on a circlet, and the regimental badge on a cloth backing in the centre. The Gloucestershire Regiment were permitted to continue wearing their back-badge, but the design was changed to the Sphinx with 'EGYPT', set in a wreath of laurel. The basic design of the helmet was the same as that of the Officers' pattern, but the peak was rounded instead of coming to a central point; the edge was bound all round with black leather; and the Other Ranks' helmet lacked the convex brass bar down the centre back. Light Infantry Regiments had helmets in dark green rather than dark blue cloth.

Senior NCOs wore straight-sided peaked forage caps; the peak had a narrow gold lace edging, and the top of the crown had a black netted central button. The band was in black oakleaf lace, except for Royal Regiments, who wore scarlet cloth bands, and Scottish Regiments, who wore diced bands. Sergeants and Other Ranks wore a dark blue Glengarry; large distinctive badges were worn by each regiment, forward on the left side, mounted on black cockades for Sergeants.

The tunic was scarlet for all ranks. It had a low standing collar with rounded fronts, and round, so-called 'jampot' cuffs, both in facing colour. The tunic was edged with white down the left front, and down the right front from waist level to the bottom edge. There were seven breast front buttons, bearing the Royal Arms; one on each shoulder strap; and two set in the rear of the waist, from which two vertical white pipings ran down the back seams to the bottom edge. The unpiped, plain scarlet shoulder straps were sewn into the shoulder seams; and were embellished in white with shortened versions of the territorial title, e.g. 'DORSET', 'OXFORD', etc. In some regiments, notably Fusiliers, initials were used instead, e.g. 'LF' or 'RF'; and in Fusilier and Light Infantry Regiments the titles were surmounted by a grenade and a bugle-horn respectively, worked in white. Until 1899 NCOs and Other Ranks of Militia Battalions had an 'M' worked in white over the title. Volunteer Battalions had cord Austrian knots over the cuffs, and white cloth stars over the right cuff indicated good conduct and long service; but Regular Regiments wore white worsted chevrons, points up above the left cuff, for this purpose.

Scarlet serge frocks were issued for wear on all Undress occasions. There were two versions. One

---

THE PLATE

Plate XXIX 2

had seven front buttons, and was prescribed for Home Service, while a five-button pattern was for use in India; in fact both types were used in the United Kingdom. The frocks had facing-colour collars, rounded skirts, and plain backs with two hip vents. Sergeants' frocks were edged in white at the front and bottom edges; and in some regiments senior NCOs had frocks trimmed with gold braid, and gold braid knots over the cuffs.

The rank of Warrant Officer was introduced in 1881, and was a War Office promotion. Garrison Sergeant Majors, Regimental Sergeant Majors, Armourer Sergeant Majors, Bandmasters, Schoolmasters, Barrack Sergeant Majors and Sergeant Instructors were all Warrant officers. Warrant Officers and Staff Sergeants had gold lace edging to the tops of their collars and cuffs. All badges of rank were of gold lace or embroidery, and were worn on the right sleeve. These were: Sergeant Major, a Crown, on the lower sleeve; Bandmaster, a silver-stringed lyre surmounted by a Crown, set on oakleaves, on the lower sleeve; Schoolmaster, no badge worn: Quartermaster Sergeant, four chevrons surmounted by an eight-point star, on the lower sleeve; Colour Sergeant, three chevrons surmounted by crossed Union Flags in coloured silks, a Crown over all, on the upper sleeve; Musketry Instructor, three chevrons with crossed rifles and a Crown over all, on the upper sleeve; Physical Training Instructor, the same but with crossed silver swords with gold hilts; Signaller and Pioneer Sergeants, three chevrons with, respectively, crossed silver and blue flags, and gold axes. Sergeants wore three gold chevrons on the upper sleeve; Lance Sergeants, three white worsted chevrons; Corporals, two white worsted chevrons; and Lance Corporals, a single white worsted chevron. General Orders laid down that all four-bar chevrons would be worn on the lower sleeve, points up, and all three-bar chevrons on the upper sleeve, points down. Sergeant Drummers (Drum Majors) wore four chevrons surmounted by a drum. All Warrant Officers, Staff Sergeants and Sergeants wore a crimson worsted sash over the right shoulder.

Signallers had crossed flags over the left cuff, the left (as viewed) flag blue, the right one white with a blue horizontal stripe. Pioneers had white crossed axes on the right upper sleeve, surmounted by a grenade or bugle-horn in Fusilier or Light Infantry Regiments respectively. Drummers' tunics were decorated over the seams with ¾in. wide white worsted lace with a repeating pattern of red Crowns; and had red wings edged and barred with similar lace, and with thick red and white cord fringes. They wore a woven drum badge on the right upper sleeve. Bandsmen had red wings edged and barred with plain white lace, and in some regiments had white lace laid over the seams of the sleeves and back. They wore a large harp, trumpet and Crown badge on the right upper sleeve.

Trousers were of dark blue cloth with a scarlet welt down each outward seam.

The Infantry were equipped with the 1871 pattern Valise Equipment. They were armed with the .45in. calibre Martini-Henry rifle adopted in 1871; in 1886 the bore was altered to .402in. and the rifling was improved. Sergeants were armed with sword bayonets instead of the socket bayonets of the rank and file. Warrant Officers and 1st Class Staff Sergeants were armed with swords which resembled the Officers' 1822 pattern, but were of lesser quality.

XXX

c1914

The Grenadier Guards

The black bearskin caps were approximately 10in. high for Other Ranks; Officers' bearskins varied in height to suit the wearer. All ranks had a white goats' hair plume fitted in a socket on the left side. The tapered chin chain of interlocking rings was backed with black leather. Officers' forage caps, of dark blue cloth, were of a special pattern with the peak edged with gold embroidery, plain black leather chin strap, and plain 1½in. wide black ribbed braid band. Other Ranks also had dark blue forage caps, with scarlet bands and scarlet pipings round the Crown. The Regimental Sergeant Major's cap had a peak bound with gold embroidery; senior NCOs' peaks were bound with brass in bands denoting rank; Lance Sergeants' and Other Ranks' cap peaks were bound with brass. Officers' cap badges were of gold embroidery; the RSM and senior NCOs had grenade badges with applied silver Crown and Royal Cyphers; Other Ranks had plain brass grenade badges.

Officers' tunics were of scarlet superfine cloth with blue cloth collars and cuffs. The collars were embroidered in gold at the front and along the top edge, and at each end bore a silver embroidered grenade set on a piece of gold lace. The round cuffs, 3¼in. deep, were embroidered in gold round the top edges. The blue cuff flaps were 6in. long at the seam and 6¾in. long at the points, 2¼in. wide at the narrowest point, and 3½in., 3⅓in. and 3¾in. wide respectively at the bottom, centre and upper points. On each 10in. deep skirt behind was a scarlet flap reaching to within ½in. of the bottom edge; there were two rear waist buttons set about 3in. apart. The fronts, collars, cuffs and cuff flaps were edged with ¼in. wide white cloth; the skirts were lined with white cloth, the shoulder straps were blue cloth, embroidered with two rows of gold purl and fastened with small buttons. There were nine front buttons set at equal distances, the lowest being of a special flat pattern to fit under the belt. Four bars of gold embroidery, with buttons, were set at equal distances on each cuff and skirt flap. Field Officers and Captains had gold embroidery around the bottom edges of their collars, and round their skirt and cuff flaps; and a second bar of embroidery around the tops of the cuffs.

There were three qualities of scarlet tunic for NCOs and junior ranks, but the basic elements were identical. Lance Sergeants, Corporals and Guardsmen had white worsted loops on the cuff and skirt flaps; buttons at equal distances; and collar and shoulder strap badges worked in white. Colour Sergeants and Sergeants had gold lace loops on the cuff and skirt flaps, and collar and shoulder strap badges worked in gold. The RSM, RQMS, Drill Sergeants and Regimental Clerks wore First Quality tunics with additional gold lace on the collar, cuff flaps and skirt flaps, around the cuffs and shoulder straps, and their collar badges were worked in silver on gold lace.

Officers' rank badges were silver Crowns and Garter Stars worked with coloured silks. The RSM wore a special badge, the full Royal Coat of Arms worked in gold, silver and coloured silks. The Colour

---

THE PLATE

FIGURES:

Top left: *Colour Sergeant, Guard Order; Corporal, Walking-Out Dress.*
Centre, left to right:
Captain, Review Order; Colonel of the Regiment, Levee Dress; Regimental Sergeant Major, Review Order.
Top right: *Sergeant, Review Order; Guardsman, Drill Order.*
Bottom left: *Company Sergeant Major, Service Dress, 1915.*
Bottom right: *Officer, Undress.*

DETAILS:

Top centre: *Officers' cap badge, above Warrant Officers' (left) and Guardsmans' cap badges, and Valise badge, set over Officers' State sash (left), Sergeants' sash and Officers' sash; RSM's sword (hilt left) and Officers' sword.*
Centre left: *RSM's badge of rank.*
Centre right: *Colour Sergeants' badge, and senior NCOs' sword knot.*
Below central figures, left to right: *RSM's locket, Sergeants' badge of rank, Other Ranks' button, Lance Sergeants' badge of rank, Guardsmens' locket.*
Schematic details, left to right: *Shoulder strap, collar, cuff flap and skirt flap details of Lieutenant; Captain and Field Officers; Senior NCOs (First Quality tunic); Sergeant; and Guardsman.*

Plate XXX 27

Badge was a representation of the crimson Royal Standard of the Regiment embroidered in gold, silver and coloured silks, surmounted by the Crown, with crossed swords beneath, set on three gold chevrons.

In Undress, Officers wore a dark blue frock coat braided in black. It was single-breasted, with five broad, point-ended black braids on the front, with corded olivets. The collar and cuffs were elaborately decorated with black tracing braid; the blue shoulder straps were edged with ½in. black braid; and the back lower skirts were also decorated with tasselled black braid with olivets at the waist. The crimson sash was worn over this coat.

In Drill Order, NCOs and junior ranks wore white serge shell jackets with brass buttons and white twisted shoulder cords.

Greatcoats were Atholl Grey. Officers' coats were double-breasted, with two rows of five regimental buttons, the space between each pair tapering in from top to waist. The NCOs' and Other Ranks' coats were single-breasted with five front buttons. The shoulder straps were of the coat material, and the cuffs were deep and round. Officers wore rank badges on the shoulder straps. NCOs wore blue-black cloth chevrons on scarlet backing cloth over the right cuff. The point of two- and three-bar chevrons and the bottom points of four-bar chevrons were 1in. above the top edge of the cuff, and the lowest parts of the Warrant Officers' badge were 6½in. from the bottom of the cuff.

At Levees, Drawing Rooms and in Evening Full Dress Officers wore blue trousers with 1½in. wide gold lace down the outward seams; for other occasions, blue trousers with 2in. wide scarlet stripes were worn. For mounted duties blue pantaloons with 2in. scarlet stripes were worn in knee boots with spurs.

On State occasions Officers wore crimson and gold sashes; on other occasions crimson silk sashes were worn. Senior NCOs wore crimson silk, and Colour Sergeants and Sergeants crimson worsted sashes, over the right shoulder.

The design of the Officers', NCOs' and Other Ranks' gilt or brass buttons was common throughout. At this period NCOs and Other Ranks wore grenade shoulder strap badges.

Officers were armed with steel-hilted swords, the half-basket guard with a distinctive grenade badge pierced and chased in the outward bars; the scabbard was steel, and the Dress sword knot of crimson and gold with a gold acorn. The Dress sword belt was of gold lace lined with Morocco leather; the Undress belt was of whitened buff leather, and the Undress knot of whitened buff leather with a gold acorn. Senior NCOs were armed with swords with steel hilts pierced with the Royal Cypher and Crown, with white leather sword knots. The RSM had a special Officers' pattern locket and fitting, and a gold sword knot with acorn. NCOs and Other Ranks were armed with the .303in. calibre Short Magazine Lee Enfield rifle and the 12in. sword bayonet.